SPECTRUM®

Math

Grade 5

Free Video Tutorials

On select pages, you will see a QR code for an instructional video that corresponds to the skill.

To access the video from your smartphone or tablet:
- Download a free QR code scanner from your device's app store.
- Launch the scanning app on your device.
- Scan the code, which will bring you to the *Spectrum Math, Grade 5* website.
- Select the video that matches the title from your workbook page.

All videos are also available at carsondellosa.com/math-5 and www.youtube.com/user/CarsonDellosaPub.

Published by Spectrum®
an imprint of Carson-Dellosa Publishing
Greensboro, NC

Spectrum®
An imprint of Carson-Dellosa Publishing LLC
P.O. Box 35665
Greensboro, NC 27425 USA

ISBN 978-1-4838-0873-4

09-172167811

Table of Contents Grade 5

Table of Contents, continued

Check What You Know

Multiplying and Dividing Whole Numbers

Multiply.

	a	b	c	d
1.	49 × 35	380 × 22	816 × 32	276 × 80
2.	2714 × 52	5216 × 16	177 × 402	818 × 321
3.	445 × 176	3420 × 634	5867 × 382	6334 × 257

Divide.

	a	b	c	d
4.	3)762	7)423	72)216	33)594
5.	24)671	63)887	45)6075	89)3299
6.	92)8147	14)3315	76)2647	17)8451

NAME _____

 Check What You Know

SHOW YOUR WORK

Multiplying and Dividing Whole Numbers

Solve each problem.

7. A video game company can fit 535 boxes of games into a truck. If the company has 47 full trucks, how many games does it have total?

The company has _____ games total.

8. Sally bought 1,425 crayons that came in packs of 15. How many packs of crayons did Sally buy?

Sally bought _____ packs.

9. Each day, 1,035 new apps are uploaded to a web server. After 28 days, how many apps would have been uploaded?

_____ apps would have been uploaded.

10. An art museum has 1,042 pictures to split equally into 45 different exhibits. How many more pictures does the museum need to make sure each exhibit has the same amount?

The museum needs _____ more pictures.

11. Robin is making bead necklaces. She wants to use 717 beads to make 57 necklaces. If she wants each necklace to have the same number of beads, how many beads will she have left over?

She will have _____ beads left over.

12. Each day, the gum ball machine in the mall sells 919 gum balls. How many gum balls would it have sold after 160 days?

It would have sold _____ gumballs.

7.

8.

9.

10.

11.

12.

Lesson 1.1 Multiplying 2 and 3 Digits by 2 Digits

Multiply right to left.

$$
\begin{array}{r}
\overset{2}{2}4 \\
\times\ \ 7 \\
\hline
168
\end{array}
$$

If $24 \times 3 = 72$, then $24 \times 30 = 720$.

$$
\begin{array}{r}
24 \\
\times\ 37 \\
\hline
168 \\
+720 \\
\hline
888
\end{array}
\qquad
\begin{array}{r}
\overset{1}{2}4 \\
\times\ 30 \\
\hline
720
\end{array}
$$

Multiply right to left.

$$
\begin{array}{r}
427 \\
\times\ \ \ 1 \\
\hline
427
\end{array}
\qquad
\begin{array}{r}
427 \\
\times\ \ 61 \\
\hline
427 \\
+25620 \\
\hline
26,047
\end{array}
\qquad
\begin{array}{r}
\overset{14}{4}27 \\
\times\ \ 60 \\
\hline
25620
\end{array}
$$

Multiply.

	a	b	c	d	e	f
1.	$\begin{array}{r}43\\ \times\ 42\end{array}$	$\begin{array}{r}75\\ \times\ 12\end{array}$	$\begin{array}{r}52\\ \times\ 28\end{array}$	$\begin{array}{r}36\\ \times\ 91\end{array}$	$\begin{array}{r}16\\ \times\ 77\end{array}$	$\begin{array}{r}21\\ \times\ 13\end{array}$
2.	$\begin{array}{r}24\\ \times\ 87\end{array}$	$\begin{array}{r}62\\ \times\ 54\end{array}$	$\begin{array}{r}96\\ \times\ 32\end{array}$	$\begin{array}{r}18\\ \times\ 47\end{array}$	$\begin{array}{r}33\\ \times\ 79\end{array}$	$\begin{array}{r}45\\ \times\ 63\end{array}$
3.	$\begin{array}{r}26\\ \times\ 53\end{array}$	$\begin{array}{r}39\\ \times\ 74\end{array}$	$\begin{array}{r}44\\ \times\ 81\end{array}$	$\begin{array}{r}473\\ \times\ 64\end{array}$	$\begin{array}{r}856\\ \times\ 22\end{array}$	$\begin{array}{r}375\\ \times\ 49\end{array}$
4.	$\begin{array}{r}838\\ \times\ 58\end{array}$	$\begin{array}{r}266\\ \times\ 93\end{array}$	$\begin{array}{r}372\\ \times\ 46\end{array}$	$\begin{array}{r}659\\ \times\ 78\end{array}$	$\begin{array}{r}428\\ \times\ 37\end{array}$	$\begin{array}{r}235\\ \times\ 86\end{array}$
5.	$\begin{array}{r}907\\ \times\ 33\end{array}$	$\begin{array}{r}415\\ \times\ 27\end{array}$	$\begin{array}{r}364\\ \times\ 82\end{array}$	$\begin{array}{r}547\\ \times\ 54\end{array}$	$\begin{array}{r}739\\ \times\ 62\end{array}$	$\begin{array}{r}697\\ \times\ 76\end{array}$

Lesson 1.2 Multiplying 4 Digits by 1 and 2 Digits

Multiply from right to left.

$2 \times 7 = 14 + 2 = 16$
$3 \times 7 = 21 + 1 = 22$

$$3236 \times 7 = 22{,}652$$

$6 \times 7 = 42$
$3 \times 7 = 21 + 4 = 25$

$$\begin{array}{r} 7198 \\ \times\ \ 14 \\ \hline 28792 \\ +\ 71980 \\ \hline 100{,}772 \end{array}$$

$$\begin{array}{r} 7198 \\ \times\ \ \ 4 \\ \hline 28792 \end{array}$$

$$\begin{array}{r} 7198 \\ \times\ \ 10 \\ \hline 71980 \end{array}$$

If $7{,}198 \times 1 = 7{,}198$,
then
$7{,}198 \times 10 = 71{,}980$.

Multiply.

	a	b	c	d	e
1.	2763×5	6204×7	3221×4	8634×8	7253×6
2.	4728×4	3962×9	1854×2	5273×6	4456×3
3.	7526×3	9428×2	3725×28	6414×37	2889×41
4.	5297×64	4175×23	8052×46	2988×85	6364×92
5.	3562×27	7451×54	1920×83	9163×72	4276×56

Lesson 1.3 Dividing 3 Digits by 2 Digits

$$71 \div 14 = 5 \qquad 18 \div 14 = 1$$
$$\text{remainder } 1 \qquad \text{remainder } 4$$

$$
\begin{array}{r}
5 \\
14\overline{)718} \\
-70 \downarrow \\
\hline
18
\end{array}
$$

$$14 \times 5 = 70 \dashrightarrow$$

$$
\begin{array}{r}
51 \\
14\overline{)718} \\
-70 \downarrow \\
\hline
18 \\
-14 \\
\hline
4
\end{array}
$$

$$
\begin{array}{r}
51 \text{ r}4 \\
14\overline{)718} \\
-70 \downarrow \\
\hline
18 \\
-14 \\
\hline
4
\end{array}
$$

The quotient is 51.
The remainder is 4.

Divide.

	a	b	c	d
1.	$23\overline{)264}$	$32\overline{)571}$	$81\overline{)724}$	$52\overline{)328}$
2.	$61\overline{)488}$	$35\overline{)175}$	$82\overline{)362}$	$47\overline{)719}$
3.	$97\overline{)891}$	$26\overline{)423}$	$43\overline{)916}$	$57\overline{)649}$

Lesson 1.4 Dividing 4 Digits by 2 Digits

$$51 \div 23 = 2 \qquad 57 \div 23 = 2 \qquad 113 \div 23 = 4$$
remainder 5   remainder 11   remainder 21

```
                    2              22            224           224 r21
                23)5173        23)5173       23)5173       23)5173
23 × 2 = 46 ----→ 46           - 46           - 46           - 46
                ————            ————          ————          ————
                   5             57            57            57
23 × 2 = 46 ------------------→ - 46          -46           -46
                               ————          ————          ————
                                113           113           113
23 × 2 = 46 ------------------------------→  - 92          - 92
                                             ————          ————
                                              21            (21)
```

The quotient is 224.
The remainder is 21.

Divide.

	a	b	c	d
1.	43)6571	22)8294	62)3628	88)4773
2.	56)2829	89)4340	75)8195	29)4872
3.	63)1890	31)6263	96)5379	48)7246

NAME _____

Lesson 1.5 Problem Solving

SHOW YOUR WORK

Solve each problem.

1. At the Bead Shop, there are 25 rows of beads. If there are 320 beads in each row, how many beads are in the shop?

   There are _____ beads in the shop.

   1.

2. The cafeteria planned to bake 3 cookies for every student in the school. If there are 715 students, how many cookies does the cafeteria need to bake?

   The cafeteria needs to bake _____ cookies.

   2.

3. A group of 123 students went on a field trip to collect seashells. If the students collected 15 shells each, how many shells did they collect?

   The students collected _____ shells.

   3.

4. A girls' club is trying to get into the record books for the most hair braids. There are 372 girls. If each girl braids her hair into 40 little braids, how many braids will they have?

   They will have _____ braids.

   4.

5. A school bought 831 boxes of computer paper for the computer lab. Each box had 59 sheets of paper inside it. How many sheets of paper were bought in total?

   The school bought _____ sheets of paper.

   5.

6. A vat of orange juice contains the juice from 231 oranges. If a company has 611 vats, how many oranges would it need to fill them all?

   The company would need _____ oranges.

   6.

Lesson 1.5 Problem Solving

Solve each problem.

1. The Pancake Restaurant served 384 pancakes. If 87 customers ate an equal number of pancakes, how many did each person eat?

   Each person ate _____ pancakes.

2. Gary opened a bag of candy containing 126 pieces. He wants to give each of his guests the same number of pieces. If he has 42 guests, how many pieces does each person get?

   Each guest gets _____ pieces.

3. At the local fair, 358 people waited in line for a boat ride. The boat can hold 8 people. How many trips will the boat have to take for everyone to get a ride?

   The boat will have to take _____ trips.

4. Cafeteria workers were putting milk cartons into crates. They had 1,052 cartons and 36 cartons in each crate. How many full crates did they end up with?

   They ended up with _____ full crates.

5. A machine in a candy company creates 9,328 pieces of candy each hour. If a box of candy has 98 pieces in it, how many boxes does the machine make in one hour?

   The machine makes _____ boxes each hour.

6. Oliver was trying to beat his old score of 1,842 points in a video game. If he scores exactly 85 points each round, how many rounds would he need to play to beat his old score?

   Oliver should play _____ rounds.

1.

2.

3.

4.

5.

6.

Check What You Learned

Multiplying and Dividing Whole Numbers

Multiply.

	a	**b**	**c**	**d**
1.	280 × 93	814 × 37	497 × 48	6492 × 82
2.	2158 × 32	8291 × 54	212 × 561	394 × 627
3.	4176 × 283	9192 × 562	7315 × 141	5639 × 374

Divide.

4. 6)2142 4)8676 49)392 34)2589

5. 72)745 45)213 61)1708 94)4649

6. 52)9243 68)3174 16)4236 81)2748

Check What You Learned | **SHOW YOUR WORK**

Multiplying and Dividing Whole Numbers

Solve each problem.

7. The park's sprinklers can spray 1,748 gallons of water on the grass in 38 minutes. How many gallons can they spray in one minute?

They can spray _____ gallons per minute.

7.

8. The auto factory will build 1,408 new trucks in the next 32 days. How many will it build in one day?

It will build _____ trucks each day.

8.

9. Pizza Depot will open 31 new restaurants next year. Each restaurant will need 27 employees. How many employees will Pizza Depot need to hire for the new restaurants?

Pizza Depot will need to hire _____ employees.

9.

10. The parking lot has 1,326 spaces to hold cars. The lot is divided into 26 equal rows. How many cars can be parked in each row?

_____ cars can park in each row.

10.

11. If a machine can make 761 pencils in a second, how many pencils can it make in 23 seconds?

It can make _____ pencils.

11.

12. In New York City, each mail truck has 1,023 pieces of junk mail. If there are 71 mail trucks, how much junk mail do they have total?

They have _____ pieces of junk mail.

12.

Check What You Know

Understanding Place Value

What is the value of the underlined digit?

	a	**b**
1.	4,3<u>3</u>2	5<u>2</u>,321

_____ _____

Write the digit that is in the given place value.

2. 30.146 – hundredth   1,325.12 – thousand

_____   _____

3. 1.325 – tenth   731.045 – one

_____   _____

Convert each power of ten to a standard number.

4. 10^4 _____ 10^6 _____

Multiply or divide by the given power of ten.

5. 8.75 × 1,000 _____   7,643 ÷ 100 _____

6. 45.67 × 1,000 _____   34,981 ÷ 1,000 _____

Write the numbers in expanded form.

7. 592,682   78.364

_____ _____

NAME _____

 Check What You Know

Understanding Place Value

Compare each pair of decimals using <, >, or =.

	a	b	c
8.	6.203 _____ 6.214	2.4 _____ 2.400	48.28 _____ 46.281
9.	72.355 _____ 72.335	5.76 _____ 50.76	9.763 _____ 9.673

Order the decimals from least to greatest.

10. 72.5, 73.943, 72.1, 73.77

_____

11. 43.2, 43.219, 42.1, 42.59

_____

12. 38.507, 38.4, 38.23, 39.5

_____

13. 71.743, 71.3, 72.43, 72.5

_____

Round each number to the indicated place.

	a	b	c
14.	3.171 – tenths	2.253 – ones	5.126 – hundredths
	_____	_____	_____
15.	64.967 – ones	9.432 – tenths	1.225 – hundredths
	_____	_____	_____

Lesson 2.1 Understanding Place Value to Millions

Write the value of the
underlined digit.
2,3<u>2</u>5,976

The value of the 2 is 2 ten
thousands, or 20,000.

Millions	Hundred Thousands	Ten Thousands	Thousands	Hundreds	Tens	Ones
2	3	<u>2</u>	5	9	7	6

Write the numerical value of the digit in the place named.

	a	b	c	d
1.	5,363,246 millions	952,418 ten thousands	4,510,367 tens	8,123,405 ones
	5,000,000	_____	_____	_____
2.	9,867,823 hundred thousands	567,345 thousands	1,328,976 millions	5,004,002 thousands
	_____	_____	_____	_____
3.	2,982,023 thousands	345,632 ten thousands	6,543,211 millions	2,566,900 hundred thousands
	_____	_____	_____	_____

Name the place of the underlined digit.

	a	b
4.	2,<u>5</u>64,740	<u>3</u>,297,134
	___ is in the _____ place.	___ is in the _____ place.
5.	8,7<u>6</u>1,089	<u>9</u>,345,187
	___ is in the _____ place.	___ is in the _____ place.
6.	<u>8</u>59,632	<u>4</u>,689,322
	___ is in the _____ place.	___ is in the _____ place.

Lesson 2.2 Understanding Place Value with Decimals

In 1,324.973 what place value is the 9?

thousands	hundreds	tens	ones	tenths	hundredths	thousandths
1	3	2	4 .	<u>9</u>	7	3

The 9 can be named nine tenths, $\frac{9}{10}$, or 0.9.

Write the place value of the given number.

	a	b	c
1.	3 in $10.03	7 in 7,000.2	5 in 13.5
2.	2 in $25.75	4 in 5,238.004	8 in 11.8
3.	1 in $561.07	3 in 0.037	6 in 0.136

Write the digit that is in the given place value.

	a	b	c	d
4.	432.14 hundreds	325.17 tenths	3,214.005 thousandths	25.132 tens
5.	30.146 hundredths	25.523 thousandths	125.043 tenths	1,325 thousands
6.	100.304 tenths	1.325 hundredths	1.005 thousandths	731.045 ones

Lesson 2.3 Powers of Ten

An **exponent** is a number that shows how many times a base number is to be used in multiplication. A **power of ten** is an exponent where the base number is always 10.

$10^1 = 1\underline{0} = 1\underline{0}$
$10^2 = 1\underline{0} \times 1\underline{0} = 1\underline{00}$
$10^3 = 1\underline{0} \times 1\underline{0} \times 1\underline{0} = 1,\underline{000}$
$10^4 = 1\underline{0} \times 1\underline{0} \times 1\underline{0} \times 1\underline{0} = 1\underline{0,000}$

Convert the values below to a power of ten.

	a	b	c
1.	100,000	1,000,000	10
	_____	_____	_____
2.	10,000,000	100	1,000,000,000
	_____	_____	_____

Convert these powers of ten to standard numbers.

	a	b	c
3.	10^7	10^5	10^3
	_____	_____	_____
4.	10^8	10^{12}	10^6
	_____	_____	_____

Lesson 2.4 Patterns of Zeros and Decimals in Products and Quotients

When a number is multiplied or divided by a multiple of 10, the number of zeros and decimals in the product or quotient will vary based on the value of the multiple of 10 that is used.

0.2658×1	=	0.2658
0.2658×10	=	2.658
0.2658×100	=	26.58
$0.2658 \times 1,000$	=	265.8
$0.2658 \times 10,000$	=	$2,658.0$
$0.2658 \times 100,000$	=	$26,580.0$
$0.2658 \times 1,000,000$	=	$265,800.0$

$265,800. \div 1$	=	$265,800.0$
$265,800. \div 10$	=	$26,580.0$
$265,800. \div 100$	=	$2,658.0$
$265,800. \div 1,000$	=	265.8
$265,800. \div 10,000$	=	26.58
$265,800. \div 100,000$	=	2.658
$265,800. \div 1,000,000$	=	0.2658

When a number is multiplied by a power of 10, the decimal in the product moves to the right and zeros are added to the left of the decimal when needed.

When a number is divided by a power of 10, the decimal in the product moves to the left and zeros are added to the right of the decimal when needed.

Multiply by the power of ten to find the product.

	a	b	c
1.	21.48×10	$6.07 \times 1,000$	7.58×100
	_____	_____	_____
2.	$7.434 \times 100,000$	$0.7 \times 1,000$	$0.502 \times 10,000$
	_____	_____	_____

Divide by the power of ten to find the quotient.

3.	$13.4 \div 10$	$27.65 \div 100$	$320.7 \div 10$
	_____	_____	_____
4.	$3.457 \div 100$	$82.93 \div 10$	$726.9 \div 1,000$
	_____	_____	_____

Lesson 2.5 Expanded Form with Whole Numbers

Expanded form is a way to write a number that shows the sum of values of each digit of a number. To use expanded form, a number has to be separated into each of its parts using place value.

5,423 = 5,000 + 400 + 20 + 3

39,572 = 30,000 + 9,000 + 500 + 70 + 2

Write each number in expanded form.

	a	b
1.	430	721
2.	3,465	43,645
3.	90,327	4,009
4.	653,410	103,254
5.	199,482	32,451
6.	9,342,751	2,500,055
7.	598,721	69,003

Lesson 2.6 Expanded Form with Decimals

Expanded form can also be used with decimals. When a number contains decimal parts, they can be separated in the same way whole number parts can.

$396.636 = 300 + 90 + 6 + 0.6 + 0.03 + 0.006$

$94,524.51 = 90,000 + 4,000 + 500 + 20 + 4 + 0.5 + 0.01$

Write each number in expanded form.

	a	b
1.	268.849	657.254
2.	182.19	9989.52
3.	756.234	332.115
4.	435.461	14.514
5.	2,948.23	69.241
6.	219.833	38,966.3
7.	519.5	971.396

Lesson 2.7 Comparing Decimals

Which is larger: 4.218 or 4.222?

4.2<u>1</u>8   4.2<u>2</u>2

The ones are the same.
The tenths are the same.
The hundredths are different.

4.218 < 4.222
4.218 is less than 4.222.

Compare each pair of decimals using <, >, or =.

	a	b	c
1.	5.213 ____ 5.312	3.1 ____ 3.10	28.35 ____ 28.251
2.	6.32 ____ 6.032	5.17 ____ 5.172	144.3 ____ 144
3.	7.325 ____ 6.425	3.14 ____ 2.99	48.28 ____ 48.280
4.	0.213 ____ 0.223	1.006 ____ 1.060	0.010 ____ 0.001
5.	0.674 ____ 0.644	3.122 ____ 3.220	43.01 ____ 43.100
6.	2.897 ____ 2.90	0.43 ____ 0.430	0.790 ____ 0.789
7.	0.571 ____ 0.58	10.462 ____ 100.46	9.36 ____ 9.306
8.	17.110 ____ 17.101	0.182 ____ 1.820	98.999 ____ 99.001
9.	1.090 ____ 1.009	25.224 ____ 25.242	63.12 ____ 63.2
10.	5.703 ____ 5.730	0.479 ____ 4.79	81.40 ____ 81.400

NAME _____

Lesson 2.8 Ordering Decimals

To order a group of decimals, line up the decimal points.

2.14, 2.08, 2.1, and 2.01

2.14
2.08
2.1
2.01

All the ones are the same. 2.14 and 2.1 have the same tenths digit, but 4 is greater than zero. In the other two numbers, 8 is greater than 1.

List from least to greatest:
2.01, 2.08, 2.1, 2.14

Order the decimals from least to greatest.

1. 7.52, 7.498, 7.521, 7.6

_____

2. 0.028, 0.080, 0.082, 0.008

_____

3. 12.193, 12.201, 12.191, 12.200

_____

4. 0.116, 0.108, 0.113, 0.117

_____

5. 22.5, 22.67, 23.8, 23.703

_____

6. 12.249, 12.13, 12.5, 12.2

_____

Lesson 2.9 Rounding to the Nearest Whole Number

Round 15.897 to the nearest whole number.

Look at the tenths digit. 15.897

8 is greater than or equal to 5, so round 5 to 6 in the ones place.

16

Round 234.054 to the nearest whole number.

Look at the tenths digit. 234.054

0 is less than 5, so keep the 4 in the ones place.

234

Round each to the nearest whole number.

	a	b	c	d
1.	6.421	5.882	19.235	2.371
2.	45.288	97.5	12.003	72.71
3.	13.936	8.42	1.100	65.39
4.	98.55	269.57	14.369	23.09
5.	95.645	8.67	99.198	51.70
6.	29.98	98.4	33.333	67.67

Lesson 2.10 Rounding Decimals

Round 2.137 to the nearest tenth.	Round 8.447 to the nearest hundredth.
Look at the hundredths digit. 2.1$\underline{3}$7	Look at the thousandths digit. 8.44$\underline{7}$
3 is less than 5, so keep the 1 in the tenths place.	7 is greater than or equal to 5, so round 4 to 5 in the hundredths place.
2.1	8.45

Round each number to the nearest tenth.

	a	b	c	d
1.	7.322	1.156	3.770	6.923
2.	7.953	4.438	5.299	8.171
3.	4.734	5.629	0.138	9.818

Round each number to the nearest hundredth.

4.	5.872	2.212	6.447	1.735
5.	4.397	4.442	9.161	3.476
6.	5.849	4.484	0.987	0.155

Check What You Learned

Understanding Place Value

What is the value of the underlined digit?

a	b

1. 83,7<u>6</u>4 _____   328.36<u>7</u> _____

Write the digit that is in the given place value.

2. 32.376 – thousandths _____   3,693.34 – hundreds _____

3. 4.398 – hundredths _____   3,982.597 – tens _____

Convert these powers of ten to standard numbers.

4. 10^9 _____ 10^5 _____

Multiply or divide by the given power of ten.

5. 532.4 × 100 _____   12.22 ÷ 10 _____

6. 4.412 × 1,000 _____   2,934.18 ÷ 100 _____

Write the numbers below in expanded form.

7. 43.436 _____   3,682.3 _____

Check What You Learned

Understanding Place Value

CHAPTER 2 POSTTEST

Compare each pair of decimals using <, >, or =.

	a	b	c
8.	5.113 ___ 5.112	42.882 ___ 43.88	4.6 ___ 4.600
9.	7.295 ___ 72.95	23.54 ___ 23.45	9.563 ___ 9.653

Order the decimals from least to greatest.

10. 5.6, 6.13, 5, 6.723

_____

11. 75.931, 75, 74.2, 74.61

_____

12. 21.1, 20.5, 21.967, 20.35

_____

13. 47.85, 46.793, 47.7, 47.5

_____

Round each number to the indicated place.

14. 7.559 – ones   2.165 – tenths   5.471 – hundredths

_____   _____   _____

15. 3.337 – hundredths   66.34 – ones   9.245 – tenths

_____   _____   _____

Lesson 3.1 Adding Decimals to Tenths

Align decimal points.

```
addend ——→    32.7
addend ——→  +  4.3
   sum ——→    37.0
```

Align decimal in sum.

To add decimals, first align the decimal point in the addends. Then, add.

Add.

	a	b	c	d
1.	0.3 + 0.6	1.1 + 1.3	2.3 + 0.4	5.2 + 4.6
2.	5.3 + 4.9	7.9 + 0.7	13.3 + 5.3	14.5 + 8.6
3.	1.0 + 0.3	88.0 + 12.4	44.1 + 2.5	30.0 + 15.7
4.	313.1 + 237.4	93.9 + 17.0	556.7 + 5.3	80.8 + 32.5
5.	0.3 0.1 + 0.0	1.4 0.2 + 0.1	32.1 8.1 + 2.0	70.0 2.1 + 0.1
6.	123.7 24.5 + 3.1	434.5 + 32.0	17.1 12.3 + 5.0	32.5 + 10.3

Lesson 3.2 Adding Decimals to Hundredths

To add decimals to hundredths, line up the decimal points. Then, add normally.

$$
\begin{array}{r} \overset{1}{26.2} \\ + 5.3 \\ \hline 31.5 \end{array}
\qquad
\begin{array}{r} \overset{1}{4.65} \\ 0.08 \\ + 7.34 \\ \hline 12.07 \end{array}
$$

Add.

	a	b	c	d
1.	3.2 + 8.5	0.73 + 0.88	1.84 + 2.39	1.44 + 8.37
2.	0.01 + 2.30	27.12 + 13.09	42.32 + 2.01	6.54 + 3.98
3.	2.72 3.51 + 4.22	68.52 1.72 + 0.55	27.15 105.21 + 2.63	7.2 8.8 + 17.5
4.	5.3 + 2.8	68.68 + 8.48	32.12 + 14.21	76.58 + 24.3
5.	6.50 + 8.72	486.25 + 103.88	168.42 + 35.69	25.09 + 3.11
6.	0.11 + 0.65	4.21 + 8.38	68.68 + 25.52	2.00 + 6.13
7.	3.16 2.12 + 1.61	0.01 1.40 + 0.50	0.23 0.60 + 0.72	4.00 2.90 + 0.02

Lesson 3.3 Subtracting Decimals to Tenths

Align decimal points.

minuend ⟶ 32.8
subtrahend ⟶ − 1.5
difference ⟶ 31.3

Align decimal points
in difference.
The difference is 31.3

> To subtract decimals, first align the decimal points in the minuend and subtrahend. Then, subtract decimals like whole numbers.

Align decimal points.

minuend ⟶ 1⁴²̸.8̸
subtrahend ⟶ − 1.9
difference ⟶ 140.9

Align decimal points
in difference.
The difference is 140.9

Subtract.

	a	b	c	d	e
1.	75.2 − 4.1	42.8 − 12.6	1.2 − 1.1	0.3 − 0.2	10.3 − 7.6
2.	576.2 − 341.1	87.0 − 1.1	1.3 − 0.1	60.4 − 7.1	117.1 − 24.0
3.	43.4 − 21.5	32.1 − 0.0	5.1 − 2.3	98.0 − 17.0	0.03 − 0.01
4.	7.8 − 0.5	52.4 − 23.8	1.9 − 0.7	0.9 − 0.0	10.1 − 8.3
5.	3.9 − 1.1	33.9 − 15.7	4.3 − 1.7	3.9 − 1.3	22.8 − 17.5
6.	2.4 − 0.2	2.9 − 0.7	58.5 − 24.9	75.0 − 18.2	183.7 − 142.9

NAME _____

Lesson 3.4 Subtracting Decimals to Hundredths

To subtract decimals to hundredths, line up the decimal points. Then, subtract normally.

$$
\begin{array}{r} 25.8 \\ -11.3 \\ \hline 14.5 \end{array}
\qquad
\begin{array}{r} {}^{31}\\ 17.\cancel{41} \\ -15.33 \\ \hline 2.08 \end{array}
$$

Subtract.

	a	b	c	d	e
1.	0.8 − 0.3	2.6 − 1.8	3.7 − 1.8	0.96 − 0.27	1.9 − 0.4
2.	18.62 − 11.58	0.45 − 0.29	0.86 − 0.53	8.6 − 7.3	11.6 − 8.8
3.	43.6 − 27.3	15.32 − 14.95	0.65 − 0.32	2.69 − 0.12	8.04 − 0.93
4.	8.45 − 4.23	27.8 − 13.4	62.43 − 38.20	14.8 − 8.9	12.68 − 4.92
5.	19.6 − 2.8	18.50 − 9.36	54.82 − 28.66	76.8 − 35.1	188.4 − 93.1
6.	14.72 − 12.86	7.40 − 5.94	4.08 − 1.39	8.6 − 7.3	5.8 − 0.9
7.	88.4 − 19.2	48.66 − 12.20	9.92 − 4.38	7.4 − 3.7	21.25 − 15.08

Lesson 3.5 Inserting Zeros to Add and Subtract

You may insert zero to help you add.

```
         1 1
0.6      0.60
0.39     0.39
+1.23   +1.23
         ____
         2.22
```

You may insert zeros to help subtract.

```
          7 1
 4.8      4.80
-2.13    -2.13
         _____
          2.67
```

Add or subtract.

	a	b	c	d	e
1.	$\begin{array}{r}2.1\\+0.25\\\hline\end{array}$	$\begin{array}{r}0.48\\+1.10\\\hline\end{array}$	$\begin{array}{r}12.7\\+3.26\\\hline\end{array}$	$\begin{array}{r}49.76\\+3.10\\\hline\end{array}$	$\begin{array}{r}5.99\\+3.25\\\hline\end{array}$
2.	$\begin{array}{r}0.87\\-0.40\\\hline\end{array}$	$\begin{array}{r}5.36\\-4.10\\\hline\end{array}$	$\begin{array}{r}3.08\\-0.72\\\hline\end{array}$	$\begin{array}{r}2.01\\+1.2\\\hline\end{array}$	$\begin{array}{r}7.4\\+2.75\\\hline\end{array}$
3.	$\begin{array}{r}14.37\\+3.00\\\hline\end{array}$	$\begin{array}{r}26.3\\+5.25\\\hline\end{array}$	$\begin{array}{r}8.81\\+0.13\\\hline\end{array}$	$\begin{array}{r}5.63\\+2.1\\\hline\end{array}$	$\begin{array}{r}6.31\\+5.80\\\hline\end{array}$
4.	$\begin{array}{r}8.3\\-2.21\\\hline\end{array}$	$\begin{array}{r}9.7\\-0.86\\\hline\end{array}$	$\begin{array}{r}18.3\\-7.26\\\hline\end{array}$	$\begin{array}{r}8.8\\+3.26\\\hline\end{array}$	$\begin{array}{r}24.2\\+5.41\\\hline\end{array}$
5.	$\begin{array}{r}4.72\\+8.50\\\hline\end{array}$	$\begin{array}{r}0.6\\+0.42\\\hline\end{array}$	$\begin{array}{r}0.92\\+4.08\\\hline\end{array}$	$\begin{array}{r}8.3\\+0.61\\\hline\end{array}$	$\begin{array}{r}2.57\\+8.80\\\hline\end{array}$
6.	$\begin{array}{r}63.2\\-5.24\\\hline\end{array}$	$\begin{array}{r}0.9\\-0.26\\\hline\end{array}$	$\begin{array}{r}102.54\\-7.68\\\hline\end{array}$	$\begin{array}{r}7.\\-4.21\\\hline\end{array}$	$\begin{array}{r}14.3\\-6.27\\\hline\end{array}$
7.	$\begin{array}{r}1.83\\4.34\\+6.20\\\hline\end{array}$	$\begin{array}{r}6.74\\8.33\\+0.2\\\hline\end{array}$	$\begin{array}{r}26.14\\-8.09\\\hline\end{array}$	$\begin{array}{r}14.1\\-8.09\\\hline\end{array}$	$\begin{array}{r}0.08\\-0.01\\\hline\end{array}$

Lesson 3.6 Problem Solving

SHOW YOUR WORK

Solve each problem.

1. Jeff wants to buy a vase for $32.75. He only has $25.15. How much does Jeff have to borrow from his brother to buy the vase?

   He has to borrow _____.

2. Booker has to pay his rent. He has $1,252.45 in the bank. His rent is $672.30. How much money will Booker have left in the bank after he pays his rent?

   Booker will have _____ left in the bank.

3. The Thomas triplets want to buy some oranges. Justin has 23 cents, Jarrod has 45 cents, and Jeremy has 52 cents. How much money do the triplets have?

   The triplets have _____.

4. A school lunch costs $1.55. Sean has $2.45. How much money will he have left after buying lunch?

   Sean will have _____.

5. Mr. Wilson just received his bill for $1,867.85 for the wedding dinner party for his daughter. His budget for the dinner was $2,000. How much less did the dinner cost than he expected?

   The dinner cost _____ less than he expected.

6. Opal is buying groceries for dinner. Ravioli costs $3.25, salad costs $1.15, and bread costs $0.35. How much do Opal's groceries cost?

   The groceries cost _____.

1.
2.
3.
4.
5.
6.

Lesson 3.7   Multiplying Decimals Using Models

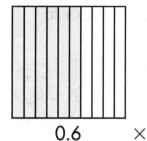  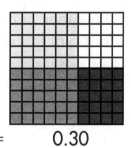

$$0.6 \quad \times \quad 0.5 \quad = \quad 0.30$$

Use models to solve the problems below.

1. $0.3 \times 0.7 =$ _____

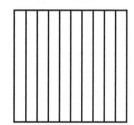 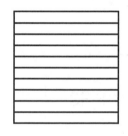 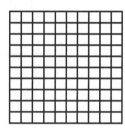

2. $0.7 \times 0.2 =$ _____

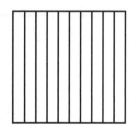 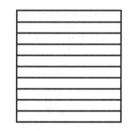 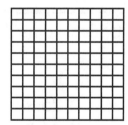

3. $0.4 \times 0.8 =$ _____

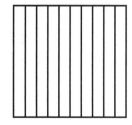 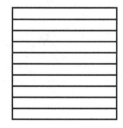 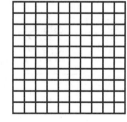

Lesson 3.8 Multiplying Decimals Using Rules

When multiplying decimals, count the number of decimal places in each factor to figure out the placement of the decimal point in the product.

$$
\begin{array}{r} 3 \\ \times\ 5 \\ \hline 15 \end{array}
\qquad
\begin{array}{r} 0.\underline{3} \\ \times\ \ 5 \\ \hline 1.5 \end{array}
\qquad
\begin{array}{r} 0.\underline{3} \\ \times\ 0.\underline{5} \\ \hline 0.15 \end{array}
\qquad
\begin{array}{r} 0.\underline{3} \\ \times\ 0.\underline{05} \\ \hline 0.015 \end{array}
$$

0 decimal places   1 decimal place   2 decimal places   3 decimal places

---

How many decimal places will be in the product of the following multiplication problems?

	a	b	c
1.	3.25×4.2	6.3×9.8	5.6×8.2
	_____	_____	_____
2.	5.3×7	9.35×8.43	2.8×7.46
	_____	_____	_____

Multiply to find the answer. Underline the decimal places in the factors and in the product.

	a	b	c	d
3.	$\begin{array}{r} 5.44 \\ \times\ 901.02 \\ \hline \end{array}$	$\begin{array}{r} 25.9 \\ \times\ 47.6 \\ \hline \end{array}$	$\begin{array}{r} 291.23 \\ \times\ \ \ 4.34 \\ \hline \end{array}$	$\begin{array}{r} 3.08 \\ \times\ 608.8 \\ \hline \end{array}$
4.	$\begin{array}{r} 908.01 \\ \times\ \ \ 4.11 \\ \hline \end{array}$	$\begin{array}{r} 92.5 \\ \times\ 50.7 \\ \hline \end{array}$	$\begin{array}{r} 901.3 \\ \times\ \ 8.2 \\ \hline \end{array}$	$\begin{array}{r} 11.4 \\ \times\ 22.4 \\ \hline \end{array}$

Lesson 3.9 Multiplication Practice

Multiply.

	a	b	c	d	e
1.	1.2 × 3	0.61 × 6	0.58 × 12	1.21 × 3	32.7 × 2
2.	3.7 × 1.5	6.24 × 2.8	3.73 × 0.77	4.38 × 0.6	1.79 × 2.5
3.	5.06 × 1.1	7.30 × 0.2	3.46 × 8.7	0.57 × 9	1.63 × 2.7
4.	6.07 × 3	5.82 × 0.4	2.10 × 1.01	4.35 × 0.8	7.42 × 6
5.	3.4 × 2	2.2 × 3.6	43.6 × 2.94	0.72 × 0.09	9.91 × 1.2

Lesson 3.10 Dividing Decimals Using Models

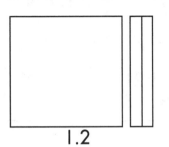 = 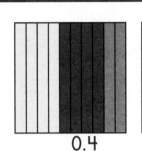 = **?**

1.2   ÷   0.4   3

Draw a hundreds block and 2 tens bars to show the number 1.2.

Divide the hundreds block into tens bars and shade each group of 4-tenths a different color.

Count the number of groups of 4 tenths. The total is your quotient.

Draw models to solve the problems.

1. $2.4 \div 0.8 =$ _____

2. $1.6 \div 0.4 =$ _____

3. $1.6 \div 0.8 =$ _____

4. $1.4 \div 0.7 =$ _____

Lesson 3.11 Dividing Decimals Using Rules

When the divisor of a division problem contains a decimal point, multiply both the divisor and the dividend by the power of ten needed to make the divisor a whole number. Then, solve the problem.

$$9.45 \div 0.9 =$$
$$(9.45 \times 10) \div (0.9 \times 10) =$$
$$94.5 \div 9 = 10.5$$

When multiplying by 10 to the first power, move the decimal point to the right one place. Add or remove zeros if necessary.

Write the power of ten needed to solve each problem. Then, solve the problem.

	a	b	c

1. $0.11\overline{)1.87}$ $0.13\overline{)1.95}$ $1.5\overline{)2.4}$

Power of 10 _____   Power of 10 _____   Power of 10 _____

2. $0.18\overline{)1.62}$ $0.12\overline{)1.56}$ $1.8\overline{)1.62}$

Power of 10 _____   Power of 10 _____   Power of 10 _____

3. $1.25\overline{)11}$ $1.3\overline{)2.34}$ $0.18\overline{)2.34}$

Power of 10 _____   Power of 10 _____   Power of 10 _____

4. $1.3\overline{)2.47}$ $0.1\overline{)1.60}$ $0.9\overline{)1.62}$

Power of 10 _____   Power of 10 _____   Power of 10 _____

Lesson 3.12 Division Practice

To make the divisor into a whole number, move the decimal point in the divisor and the dividend the same number of places to the right.

$$1.5 \overline{)40.5} = 15 \overline{)405} \qquad 1.05 \overline{)24.15} = 105 \overline{)2415}$$

$$
\begin{array}{r}
27 \\
15 \overline{)405} \\
-30 \\
\hline
105 \\
-105 \\
\hline
0
\end{array}
\qquad
\begin{array}{r}
23 \\
105 \overline{)2415} \\
-210 \\
\hline
315 \\
-315 \\
\hline
0
\end{array}
$$

Divide.

	a	b	c	d
1.	$0.03 \overline{)45.6}$	$1.7 \overline{)20.4}$	$3.8 \overline{)16.72}$	$0.5 \overline{)1.87}$
2.	$7.4 \overline{)28.86}$	$1.07 \overline{)67.41}$	$0.22 \overline{)8.03}$	$0.15 \overline{)0.99}$
3.	$0.08 \overline{)2.52}$	$0.02 \overline{)6.56}$	$1.5 \overline{)8.4}$	$6.4 \overline{)27.04}$
4.	$0.65 \overline{)0.91}$	$0.08 \overline{)0.17}$	$0.17 \overline{)3.06}$	$2.1 \overline{)3.36}$

Lesson 3.13 Problem Solving

SHOW YOUR WORK

Solve each problem.

1. Fred bought 7 games on clearance for $104.65. Each game was on sale for the same price. How much did each game cost?

   Each game cost _____.

2. Gas costs $1.64 a gallon. Elaine spent $23.78 at the gas station. How many gallons of gas did she buy?

   Elaine bought _____ gallons of gas.

3. There are 2.5 servings in a can of tuna fish. How many servings are there in 7 cans?

   There are _____ servings in 7 cans.

4. A grain distributor can process 14.6 tons of grain an hour. How much can the distributor process in 8.75 hours?

   The distributor can process _____ tons of grain.

5. Rhonda earned $324.65 delivering newspapers. She promised her sister 0.2 of her earnings for helping her. How much does Rhonda owe her sister?

   Rhonda owes her sister _____.

6. A car traveled 48.36 miles in one hour. What was its average speed per minute?

   Its average speed was _____ miles per minute.

7. There are 5.28 cups of pudding to be put into 6 dishes. How much pudding should be put into each dish to make them equal?

   Each dish should get _____ cups of pudding.

1.

2.

3.

4.

5.

6.

7.

Check What You Learned

Using Decimals

CHAPTER 3 POSTTEST

Add or subtract.

	a	b	c	d
1.	0.23 + 0.9	78.07 + 1.34	9.06 + 2.78	48.78 + 9.03
2.	29.08 − 2.10	13.73 − 8.64	3.89 − 1.47	33.04 − 6.75
3.	0.98 + 0.87	26.32 + 1.14	42.55 − 3.75	81.12 + 56.29

Multiply or divide.

	a	b	c	d
4.	6.2 × 0.4	3.05 × 2.83	5.73 × 2.83	4.03 × 1.1

5.   0.25)‾65‾   0.04)‾19‾   0.7)‾13.23‾   1.3)‾2.86‾

Check What You Learned

Using Decimals

Solve each problem.

6. Sheila bought three books for $12.63, $9.05, and $14.97. How much did she spend?

Sheila spent _____ on the three books.

6.

7. Roberto bought a 12-pack of bottled water. Each bottle held 0.75 liters. How many liters of water did he buy?

Roberto bought _____ liters.

7.

8. The highest batting average on the Owls baseball team is 0.42. The lowest batting average is 0.18. What is the difference?

The difference is _____.

8.

9. Lou spent $17.65 to buy 5 items of equal value. How much did he spend on each item?

Lou spent _____ on each item.

9.

10. A hike is 26.4 miles. Alicia wants to divide it equally over 3 days. How far does she need to hike each day?

She needs to hike _____ miles each day.

10.

11. There are 6.75 buckets of sand in a sandbox. If each full bucket holds 4.32 pounds of sand, how many pounds of sand are there in the sandbox?

There are _____ pounds of sand in the sandbox.

11.

Check What You Know

Understanding Fractions

Change each improper fraction to a mixed number.

	a	b	c	d	e
1.	$\frac{27}{5}$ _____	$\frac{35}{8}$ _____	$\frac{15}{7}$ _____	$\frac{25}{4}$ _____	$\frac{17}{3}$ _____

Change each mixed number to an improper fraction.

2.	$3\frac{5}{16}$ _____	$3\frac{3}{5}$ _____	$2\frac{3}{7}$ _____	$1\frac{3}{16}$ _____	$4\frac{1}{3}$ _____

Find the greatest common factor for each set of numbers.

3.	18 and 22	25 and 50	54 and 36	40 and 8	16 and 24
	_____	_____	_____	_____	_____
4.	10 and 15	24 and 30	8 and 10	5 and 24	24 and 40
	_____	_____	_____	_____	_____

Find the least common multiple for each set of numbers.

5.	8 and 12	15 and 4	20 and 4	3 and 24	12 and 4
	_____	_____	_____	_____	_____
6.	15 and 2	12 and 30	4 and 30	6 and 40	10 and 2
	_____	_____	_____	_____	_____

Check What You Know

Understanding Fractions

Write each fraction in simplest form.

	a	**b**	**c**	**d**

7. $\dfrac{6}{9}$ _____ $\dfrac{12}{36}$ _____ $\dfrac{20}{32}$ _____ $\dfrac{21}{49}$ _____

8. $\dfrac{15}{18}$ _____ $\dfrac{40}{45}$ _____ $\dfrac{12}{14}$ _____ $\dfrac{19}{38}$ _____

Find the equivalent fraction.

9. $\dfrac{4}{6}=\dfrac{}{12}$ $\dfrac{1}{9}=\dfrac{}{18}$ $\dfrac{5}{6}=\dfrac{}{12}$ $\dfrac{5}{12}=\dfrac{}{60}$

10. $\dfrac{2}{5}=\dfrac{}{20}$ $7=\dfrac{}{6}$ $6=\dfrac{}{11}$ $4=\dfrac{}{7}$

Compare each pair of fractions using $<$, $>$, or $=$.

11. $\dfrac{8}{12}$ ___ $\dfrac{1}{12}$ $\dfrac{2}{3}$ ___ $\dfrac{1}{2}$ $\dfrac{6}{9}$ ___ $\dfrac{2}{5}$ $\dfrac{4}{6}$ ___ $\dfrac{5}{9}$

12. $\dfrac{3}{6}$ ___ $\dfrac{7}{9}$ $\dfrac{2}{5}$ ___ $\dfrac{1}{4}$ $\dfrac{2}{7}$ ___ $\dfrac{2}{3}$ $\dfrac{6}{7}$ ___ $\dfrac{1}{5}$

Convert each fraction into a decimal. Convert each decimal into a fraction.

13. $\dfrac{2}{5}$ _____ $\dfrac{3}{6}$ _____ $\dfrac{2}{8}$ _____ $\dfrac{7}{8}$ _____

14. 0.5 _____   0.6 _____   0.75 _____   0.625 _____

Lesson 4.1 Fractions and Division

Fractions tell how items are divided. When you see a fraction written like this, $\frac{1}{3}$, that means something has been divided into 3 parts and the fraction is one of those parts. The division problem $1 \div 3$, gives the same result.

Read each problem and then answer the questions.

1. If you have 3 pies, and you want to split them between 4 people, how much pie will each person receive?

   Each pie will be cut into _____ pieces.

   Each person will receive _____ of a pie.

2. A 45-pound bag of rice is going to be split between 5 families. How much rice will each family receive?

   The way to write this as a division problem is _____ .

   The way to write this as a fraction is _____ .

   Each family will receive _____ pounds of rice.

3. A group of 3 students has to read a 21-page chapter for homework. How many pages will each student have to read if they are sharing the load?

   The way to write this as a division problem is _____ .

   The way to write this as a fraction is _____ .

   Each student will need to read _____ pages of the chapter.

4. John bought two 5-pound bags of candy to share with his classmates. If there are 25 students in John's class, how much candy will each student receive?

   Each bag of candy will be split _____ ways.

   Each person will receive _____ pounds of candy.

Lesson 4.2 Changing Improper Fractions to Mixed Numbers

$\frac{13}{6}$ means $13 \div 6$ or $6\overline{)13}$

$$6\overline{)13} \quad \begin{array}{r} 2\frac{1}{6} \\ \hline \end{array}$$
$$-12$$
$$1 \longrightarrow 1 \div 6 = \boxed{\frac{1}{6}}$$

So, $\frac{13}{6} = 2\frac{1}{6}$

$\frac{13}{6}$ is an **improper fraction**, meaning the denominator divides the numerator at least one time. In other words, the numerator is greater than the denominator.

$2\frac{1}{6}$ is a **mixed number**. This is the simplest form of an improper fraction.

Write each improper fraction as a mixed number in simplest form.

	a	b	c
1.	$\frac{5}{3}$ _____	$\frac{7}{6}$ _____	$\frac{9}{5}$ _____
2.	$\frac{3}{2}$ _____	$\frac{4}{3}$ _____	$\frac{8}{5}$ _____
3.	$\frac{7}{5}$ _____	$\frac{9}{7}$ _____	$\frac{5}{4}$ _____
4.	$\frac{32}{6}$ _____	$\frac{51}{4}$ _____	$\frac{49}{9}$ _____
5.	$\frac{66}{5}$ _____	$\frac{83}{3}$ _____	$\frac{28}{5}$ _____
6.	$\frac{29}{3}$ _____	$\frac{28}{7}$ _____	$\frac{64}{6}$ _____

Lesson 4.3 Changing Mixed Numbers to Improper Fractions

To change a mixed number to a fraction, multiply the denominator by the whole number. Then, add the numerator to the product to get the new numerator. Keep the denominator the same.

$$4\frac{3}{5} = \frac{(5 \times 4) + 3}{5} = \frac{20 + 3}{5} = \frac{23}{5} \qquad 2\frac{3}{4} = \frac{(4 \times 2) + 3}{4} = \frac{8 + 3}{4} = \frac{11}{4}$$

Change each mixed number to an improper fraction.

	a	b	c	d
1.	$2\frac{5}{8}$ _____	$3\frac{1}{4}$ _____	$2\frac{3}{7}$ _____	$4\frac{1}{1}$ _____
2.	$3\frac{3}{4}$ _____	$2\frac{5}{12}$ _____	$4\frac{1}{6}$ _____	$5\frac{2}{3}$ _____
3.	$2\frac{7}{16}$ _____	$3\frac{1}{2}$ _____	$1\frac{7}{16}$ _____	$2\frac{5}{8}$ _____
4.	$3\frac{1}{3}$ _____	$4\frac{2}{5}$ _____	$3\frac{1}{8}$ _____	$7\frac{1}{3}$ _____
5.	$8\frac{2}{3}$ _____	$1\frac{2}{5}$ _____	$2\frac{3}{7}$ _____	$3\frac{8}{9}$ _____
6.	$4\frac{2}{5}$ _____	$3\frac{5}{6}$ _____	$2\frac{4}{9}$ _____	$4\frac{5}{12}$ _____

Lesson 4.4 Reviewing Factors and Multiples

Greatest Common Factor

Find the greatest common factor by looking for which factors two numbers share and then figure out which is the greatest.

$8 - 1, 2, 4, 8$
$16 - 1, 2, 4, 8, 16$ } The greatest common factor is 8

Least Common Multiple

Find the least common multiple by listing multiples of each number until finding the first one that is shared.

$3 - 3, 6, 9, 12$
$4 - 4, 8, 12$ } The least common multiple is 12

Find the greatest common factor of these numbers.

	a	b
1.	14 and 42 _____	27 and 18 _____
2.	36 and 24 _____	45 and 20 _____
3.	72 and 54 _____	42 and 49 _____
4.	86 and 94 _____	66 and 11 _____

Find the least common multiple of these numbers.

5.	2 and 7 _____	4 and 10 _____
6.	4 and 5 _____	6 and 10 _____
7.	4 and 12 _____	6 and 18 _____
8.	2 and 5 _____	5 and 11 _____

Lesson 4.5 Finding Common Denominators

The two fractions $\frac{1}{5}$ and $\frac{3}{5}$ have common denominators. However $\frac{1}{4}$ and $\frac{3}{5}$ do not have common denominators. Rename these fractions so that they have common denominators by finding the least common multiple of their denominators.

Multiples of 4 are 4, 8, 12, 16, 20, 24, . . .

Multiples of 5 are 5, 10, 15, 20, . . .

The smallest number that is a multiple of 4 and 5 is 20.

Rename each fraction with a denominator of 20.

$\frac{1}{4} = \frac{1 \times 5}{4 \times 5} = \frac{5}{20}; \frac{3}{5} = \frac{3 \times 4}{5 \times 4} = \frac{12}{20}$

$\frac{5}{20}$ and $\frac{12}{20}$ have common denominators.

Rename each pair of fractions with common denominators.

	a	b	c
1.	$\frac{1}{4}$ and $\frac{2}{3}$ _____	$\frac{3}{8}$ and $\frac{7}{10}$ _____	$\frac{4}{7}$ and $\frac{2}{3}$ _____
2.	$\frac{3}{8}$ and $\frac{1}{6}$ _____	$\frac{2}{3}$ and $\frac{1}{2}$ _____	$\frac{3}{8}$ and $\frac{5}{6}$ _____
3.	$\frac{2}{5}$ and $\frac{1}{3}$ _____	$\frac{5}{16}$ and $\frac{3}{8}$ _____	$\frac{1}{2}$ and $\frac{1}{3}$ _____
4.	$\frac{5}{8}$ and $\frac{3}{16}$ _____	$\frac{2}{5}$ and $\frac{3}{4}$ _____	$\frac{5}{12}$ and $\frac{4}{5}$ _____
5.	$\frac{5}{9}$ and $\frac{1}{2}$ _____	$\frac{7}{8}$ and $\frac{7}{12}$ _____	$\frac{1}{9}$ and $\frac{2}{3}$ _____

Lesson 4.6 Finding Equivalent Fractions

$8 = \dfrac{\square}{4}$

$8 = \dfrac{8}{1}$ Rewrite the whole number as a fraction whose denominator is one.

$\dfrac{8}{1} \times \dfrac{4}{4} = \dfrac{32}{4}$ Multiply the numerator and denominator by the same number.

$8 = \dfrac{32}{4}$ $\dfrac{8}{1}$ and $\dfrac{32}{4}$ are equivalent fractions.

Find the equivalent fraction.

	a	b	c
1.	$\dfrac{1}{3} = \dfrac{}{6}$	$\dfrac{3}{5} = \dfrac{}{15}$	$\dfrac{2}{9} = \dfrac{}{27}$
2.	$\dfrac{6}{7} = \dfrac{}{14}$	$2 = \dfrac{}{3}$	$5 = \dfrac{}{7}$
3.	$7 = \dfrac{}{5}$	$\dfrac{5}{8} = \dfrac{}{24}$	$1 = \dfrac{}{6}$
4.	$3 = \dfrac{}{9}$	$\dfrac{8}{11} = \dfrac{}{33}$	$\dfrac{5}{6} = \dfrac{}{30}$
5.	$6 = \dfrac{}{3}$	$\dfrac{7}{9} = \dfrac{}{18}$	$8 = \dfrac{}{6}$

Lesson 4.7 Simplifying Fractions

$$\frac{12}{16} \div \frac{4}{4} = \frac{3}{4} \qquad \frac{12}{16} = \frac{3}{4}$$

$$\frac{36}{72} \div \frac{36}{36} = \frac{1}{2} \qquad \frac{36}{72} = \frac{1}{2}$$

To reduce a fraction to its simplest form, divide the numerator and denominator by the same number. The fraction is in simplest form when 1 is the only common factor.

Reduce each fraction to simplest form.

	a	b	c
1.	$\frac{3}{6}$ _____	$\frac{5}{10}$ _____	$\frac{9}{18}$ _____
2.	$\frac{6}{24}$ _____	$\frac{4}{12}$ _____	$\frac{2}{10}$ _____
3.	$\frac{4}{20}$ _____	$\frac{12}{15}$ _____	$\frac{8}{32}$ _____
4.	$\frac{18}{36}$ _____	$\frac{26}{28}$ _____	$\frac{17}{68}$ _____
5.	$\frac{25}{35}$ _____	$\frac{51}{75}$ _____	$\frac{28}{36}$ _____
6.	$\frac{22}{64}$ _____	$\frac{49}{63}$ _____	$\frac{24}{96}$ _____

Lesson 4.8 Simplifying Mixed Numbers

A mixed numeral is in simplest form if its fraction is in simplest form and names a number less than 1.

The greatest common factor of 8 and 12 is 4.

$$3\frac{8}{12}$$

$$3 + \frac{8 \div 4}{12 \div 4} = \frac{2}{3}$$

$$3\frac{8}{12} = 3\frac{2}{3}$$

$$2\frac{9}{4} = 2 + \frac{9}{4}$$

$$\uparrow \quad 2 + (2\frac{1}{4}) = 4\frac{1}{4}$$

not in simplest form

Reduce each mixed numeral to simplest form.

	a	b	c	d
1.	$3\frac{6}{8}$ _____	$2\frac{12}{15}$ _____	$1\frac{9}{12}$ _____	$4\frac{10}{15}$ _____
2.	$2\frac{8}{5}$ _____	$3\frac{15}{4}$ _____	$1\frac{7}{3}$ _____	$2\frac{5}{2}$ _____
3.	$4\frac{4}{8}$ _____	$5\frac{6}{9}$ _____	$8\frac{12}{20}$ _____	$7\frac{4}{16}$ _____
4.	$2\frac{10}{4}$ _____	$3\frac{3}{2}$ _____	$7\frac{8}{12}$ _____	$5\frac{3}{9}$ _____
5.	$2\frac{10}{3}$ _____	$4\frac{6}{5}$ _____	$3\frac{15}{7}$ _____	$2\frac{20}{9}$ _____

Lesson 4.9 Comparing and Ordering Fractions

Use your knowledge of simplifying, finding common denominators, and finding equivalent fractions.

Compare each pair of fractions using $<$, $>$, or $=$.

	a	b	c	d
1.	$\frac{19}{9}$ ___ $\frac{1}{10}$	$1\frac{1}{12}$ ___ $10\frac{1}{3}$	$2\frac{1}{9}$ ___ $10\frac{1}{2}$	$\frac{1}{9}$ ___ $\frac{6}{7}$
2.	$\frac{4}{6}$ ___ $\frac{5}{9}$	$\frac{4}{7}$ ___ $\frac{21}{11}$	$\frac{29}{9}$ ___ $2\frac{1}{6}$	$\frac{26}{11}$ ___ $\frac{22}{11}$
3.	$\frac{20}{8}$ ___ $\frac{12}{8}$	$\frac{4}{9}$ ___ $7\frac{1}{4}$	$2\frac{11}{12}$ ___ $1\frac{1}{5}$	$\frac{4}{2}$ ___ $\frac{29}{9}$
4.	$\frac{2}{2}$ ___ $\frac{1}{3}$	$\frac{1}{3}$ ___ $2\frac{11}{12}$	$5\frac{1}{2}$ ___ $\frac{11}{12}$	$\frac{13}{3}$ ___ $\frac{1}{5}$
5.	$\frac{2}{5}$ ___ $2\frac{3}{8}$	$\frac{20}{11}$ ___ $\frac{25}{2}$	$\frac{1}{7}$ ___ $7\frac{1}{3}$	$\frac{1}{9}$ ___ $\frac{19}{6}$
6.	$3\frac{2}{10}$ ___ $\frac{26}{8}$	$\frac{2}{3}$ ___ $\frac{1}{2}$	$\frac{5}{9}$ ___ $\frac{1}{9}$	$\frac{19}{9}$ ___ $\frac{27}{4}$

Put the fractions in order from least to greatest.

7. $\frac{1}{7}$, $\frac{6}{7}$, $1\frac{2}{3}$, $1\frac{8}{9}$, $1\frac{1}{7}$

_____

8. $\frac{7}{8}$, $\frac{4}{7}$, $1\frac{1}{2}$, $\frac{2}{7}$, $1\frac{1}{4}$

_____

9. $\frac{5}{6}$, $1\frac{4}{7}$, $\frac{1}{6}$, $1\frac{1}{3}$, $1\frac{7}{8}$

_____

Lesson 4.10 Changing Fractions to Decimals

Change $\frac{1}{5}$ to tenths.

$\frac{1}{5} = \frac{1 \times 2}{5 \times 2} = \frac{2}{10} = 0.2$

Change $\frac{1}{5}$ to hundredths.

$\frac{1}{5} = \frac{1 \times 20}{5 \times 20} = \frac{20}{100} = 0.20$

Change $\frac{1}{4}$ to hundredths.

$\frac{1}{4} = \frac{1 \times 25}{4 \times 25} = \frac{25}{100} = 0.25$

Change $3\frac{1}{250}$ to thousandths.

$3\frac{1}{250} = 3\frac{1 \times 4}{250 \times 4} = 3\frac{4}{1000} = 3.004$

Change each of the following to a decimal as indicated.

	a	b	c
1.	Change $\frac{2}{5}$ to tenths.	Change $\frac{2}{5}$ to hundredths.	Change $\frac{2}{5}$ to thousandths.
2.	Change $3\frac{1}{2}$ to tenths.	Change $\frac{3}{25}$ to hundredths.	Change $\frac{17}{25}$ to thousandths.
3.	Change $2\frac{3}{5}$ to tenths.	Change $\frac{9}{20}$ to hundredths.	Change $\frac{29}{250}$ to thousandths.
4.	Change $2\frac{1}{5}$ to tenths.	Change $\frac{17}{50}$ to hundredths.	Change $1\frac{27}{100}$ to thousandths.
5.	Change $\frac{4}{5}$ to tenths.	Change $\frac{3}{4}$ to hundredths.	Change $\frac{3}{40}$ to thousandths.
6.	Change $7\frac{1}{2}$ to tenths.	Change $2\frac{3}{10}$ to hundredths.	Change $\frac{7}{125}$ to thousandths.

Lesson 4.11 Changing Decimals to Fractions

$0.4 = \frac{4}{10} = \frac{2}{5}$

$0.19 = \frac{19}{100}$

$2.35 = 2\frac{35}{100} = 2\frac{7}{20}$

$0.125 = \frac{125}{1000} = \frac{1}{8}$

$3.24 = 3\frac{24}{100} = 3\frac{6}{20}$

Write each decimal as a fraction or mixed number in simplest form.

	a	b	c	d
1.	0.4 _____	0.75 _____	3.1 _____	0.6 _____
2.	0.25 _____	1.3 _____	4.15 _____	2.2 _____
3.	3.125 _____	0.16 _____	8.4 _____	2.5 _____
4.	0.001 _____	0.04 _____	1.6 _____	1.01 _____
5.	0.64 _____	0.70 _____	4.6 _____	0.88 _____
6.	2.42 _____	0.56 _____	0.15 _____	0.002 _____
7.	2.3 _____	3.9 _____	1.95 _____	0.442 _____
8.	1.86 _____	3.31 _____	0.96 _____	0.12 _____
9.	4.76 _____	3.89 _____	4.08 _____	0.55 _____

Check What You Learned

Understanding Fractions

hange each improper fraction to a mixed number in simplest form.

	a	b	c	d	e
1.	$\dfrac{22}{4}$ _____	$\dfrac{9}{8}$ _____	$\dfrac{17}{6}$ _____	$\dfrac{23}{9}$ _____	$\dfrac{26}{12}$ _____
2.	$\dfrac{48}{21}$ _____	$\dfrac{25}{3}$ _____	$\dfrac{10}{7}$ _____	$\dfrac{30}{7}$ _____	$\dfrac{22}{8}$ _____

hange each mixed number to an improper fraction.

3.	$3\dfrac{6}{8}$ _____	$9\dfrac{8}{12}$ _____	$4\dfrac{7}{14}$ _____	$6\dfrac{3}{8}$ _____	$2\dfrac{9}{8}$ _____
4.	$2\dfrac{3}{4}$ _____	$6\dfrac{8}{9}$ _____	$8\dfrac{11}{12}$ _____	$4\dfrac{4}{9}$ _____	$5\dfrac{2}{7}$ _____

Find the greatest common factor for each set of numbers.

5.	16 and 24	21 and 14	9 and 45	13 and 25	12 and 45
	_____	_____	_____	_____	_____

Find the least common multiple for each set of numbers.

6.	3 and 4	4 and 12	15 and 20	10 and 6	10 and 3
	_____	_____	_____	_____	_____

Check What You Learned

Understanding Fractions

Write each fraction in simplest form.

a	b	c	d
7. $\frac{10}{25}$ _____	$\frac{21}{35}$ _____	$\frac{15}{24}$ _____	$\frac{16}{20}$ _____
8. $\frac{21}{24}$ _____	$\frac{6}{21}$ _____	$\frac{20}{32}$ _____	$\frac{48}{54}$ _____

Find the equivalent fraction.

9. $\frac{7}{12} = \frac{}{60}$ $\frac{8}{9} = \frac{}{81}$ $4 = \frac{}{8}$ $\frac{7}{10} = \frac{}{30}$

10. $7 = \frac{}{7}$ $\frac{5}{11} = \frac{}{33}$ $3 = \frac{}{6}$ $9 = \frac{}{4}$

Compare each pair of fractions using $<$, $>$, or $=$.

11. $\frac{8}{6}$ ____ $\frac{6}{8}$ $\frac{10}{8}$ ____ $\frac{6}{5}$ $\frac{7}{9}$ ____ $\frac{6}{8}$ $\frac{12}{10}$ ____ $\frac{6}{5}$

12. $\frac{4}{6}$ ____ $\frac{10}{5}$ $\frac{6}{7}$ ____ $\frac{5}{6}$ $\frac{8}{5}$ ____ $\frac{10}{8}$ $\frac{4}{9}$ ____ $\frac{4}{5}$

Convert each fraction into a decimal. Convert each decimal into a fraction.

13. $\frac{8}{20}$ _____ $\frac{3}{5}$ _____ $\frac{7}{14}$ _____ $\frac{9}{30}$ _____

14. 7.26 _____   10.4 _____   0.7 _____   6.25 _____

Check What You Know

Adding and Subtracting Fractions

Write each fraction in simplest form.

	a	b	c	d

1.

a. $\dfrac{1}{8} + \dfrac{6}{8}$

b. $\dfrac{3}{7} + \dfrac{3}{7}$

c. $\dfrac{2}{6} + \dfrac{1}{6}$

d. $\dfrac{4}{9} + \dfrac{3}{9}$

2.

a. $\dfrac{4}{5} + \dfrac{2}{8}$

b. $\dfrac{3}{6} + \dfrac{2}{4}$

c. $4\dfrac{2}{3} + 7\dfrac{2}{9}$

d. $1\dfrac{4}{5} + 6\dfrac{1}{8}$

3.

a. $\dfrac{7}{8} - \dfrac{1}{8}$

b. $\dfrac{5}{9} - \dfrac{4}{9}$

c. $\dfrac{8}{10} - \dfrac{3}{10}$

d. $\dfrac{7}{12} - \dfrac{1}{12}$

4.

a. $\dfrac{7}{8} - \dfrac{3}{4}$

b. $\dfrac{6}{7} - \dfrac{4}{5}$

c. $\dfrac{4}{7} - \dfrac{2}{9}$

d. $6\dfrac{1}{4} - 2\dfrac{1}{6}$

Check What You Know

Adding and Subtracting Fractions

Solve each problem.

5. Julianne needs 7 yards of string for her kite. She has $\frac{5}{8}$ yards. How many more yards does Julianne need for her kite?

Julianne needs _____ more yards of string.

5.

6. Mrs. Thompson's cookie recipe includes $\frac{1}{3}$ cup sugar and 4 cups flour. How many cups of sugar and flour does Mrs. Thompson need for her cookies?

Mrs. Thompson needs _____ cups of ingredients.

6.

7. Marlon watched a movie $1\frac{8}{9}$ hours long. Jessie watched a movie $2\frac{2}{7}$ hours long. How much longer was Jessie's movie than Marlon's?

Jessie's movie was _____ hours longer.

7.

8. Carrie is running in a track meet. In one race she must run $\frac{1}{4}$ mile, and in a second race she must run $1\frac{2}{5}$ miles. How many miles must Carrie run in all?

Carrie must run _____ miles.

8.

9. David practiced soccer twice last week. On Monday, he practiced $2\frac{1}{3}$ hours. On Wednesday, he practiced $1\frac{7}{9}$ hours. How much longer did David practice on Monday?

David practiced _____ hours longer on Monday.

9.

Lesson 5.2 Adding Fractions with Unlike Denominators

Add. Write answers in simplest form.

	a	b	c	d	e
1.	$\frac{1}{2}$ $+ \frac{3}{4}$	$\frac{3}{3}$ $+ \frac{1}{10}$	$\frac{5}{6}$ $+ \frac{3}{4}$	$\frac{1}{3}$ $+ \frac{5}{6}$	$\frac{2}{3}$ $+ \frac{1}{12}$
2.	$\frac{3}{8}$ $+ \frac{1}{4}$	$\frac{2}{3}$ $+ \frac{5}{9}$	$\frac{5}{12}$ $+ \frac{7}{8}$	$\frac{1}{2}$ $+ \frac{7}{10}$	$\frac{3}{4}$ $+ \frac{5}{6}$
3.	$\frac{5}{7}$ $+ \frac{4}{14}$	$\frac{1}{6}$ $+ \frac{7}{8}$	$\frac{9}{10}$ $+ \frac{5}{8}$	$\frac{2}{9}$ $+ \frac{11}{12}$	$\frac{5}{6}$ $+ \frac{8}{9}$
4.	$\frac{3}{5}$ $+ \frac{1}{10}$	$\frac{3}{5}$ $+ \frac{9}{10}$	$\frac{1}{4}$ $+ \frac{5}{6}$	$\frac{3}{8}$ $+ \frac{1}{12}$	$\frac{2}{5}$ $+ \frac{2}{7}$

Lesson 5.3 Subtracting Fractions with Unlike Denominators

$$\begin{array}{rcl} \frac{2}{3} \times \frac{7}{7} &=& \frac{14}{21} \\[6pt] -\frac{2}{7} \times \frac{3}{3} &=& -\frac{6}{21} \\[6pt] \hline && \frac{8}{21} \end{array}$$

When subtracting fractions that have different denominators, rename fractions to have a common denominator. Then, subtract fractions, and write the difference in simplest form.

$$\begin{array}{rcl} \frac{5}{6} \times \frac{1}{1} &=& \frac{5}{6} \\[6pt] -\frac{2}{3} \times \frac{2}{2} &=& -\frac{4}{6} \\[6pt] \hline && \frac{1}{6} \end{array}$$

Subtract. Write answers in simplest form.

	a	b	c	d	e
1.	$\frac{3}{4}$ $-\frac{1}{2}$	$\frac{5}{6}$ $-\frac{1}{3}$	$\frac{9}{10}$ $-\frac{2}{5}$	$\frac{4}{7}$ $-\frac{1}{8}$	$\frac{5}{9}$ $-\frac{1}{3}$
2.	$\frac{2}{5}$ $-\frac{1}{9}$	$\frac{3}{5}$ $-\frac{2}{7}$	$\frac{2}{3}$ $-\frac{3}{8}$	$\frac{5}{6}$ $-\frac{1}{3}$	$\frac{3}{4}$ $-\frac{2}{9}$
3.	$\frac{7}{10}$ $-\frac{3}{6}$	$\frac{8}{9}$ $-\frac{1}{4}$	$\frac{7}{8}$ $-\frac{5}{12}$	$\frac{7}{10}$ $-\frac{1}{4}$	$\frac{4}{5}$ $-\frac{3}{7}$

Lesson 5.3 Subtracting Fractions with Unlike Denominators

Subtract. Write answers in simplest form.

	a	b	c	d
1.	$\dfrac{5}{9}$ $-\dfrac{5}{18}$	$\dfrac{5}{8}$ $-\dfrac{3}{12}$	$\dfrac{7}{18}$ $-\dfrac{3}{9}$	$\dfrac{4}{8}$ $-\dfrac{7}{16}$
2.	$\dfrac{5}{10}$ $-\dfrac{1}{15}$	$\dfrac{9}{18}$ $-\dfrac{2}{15}$	$\dfrac{9}{10}$ $-\dfrac{9}{14}$	$\dfrac{6}{16}$ $-\dfrac{1}{8}$
3.	$\dfrac{5}{8}$ $-\dfrac{1}{9}$	$\dfrac{7}{10}$ $-\dfrac{7}{15}$	$\dfrac{8}{36}$ $-\dfrac{3}{14}$	$\dfrac{13}{36}$ $-\dfrac{9}{35}$
4.	$\dfrac{10}{25}$ $-\dfrac{2}{9}$	$\dfrac{5}{24}$ $-\dfrac{3}{15}$	$\dfrac{1}{8}$ $-\dfrac{3}{26}$	$\dfrac{9}{14}$ $-\dfrac{1}{8}$

Lesson 5.4 Adding Mixed Numbers

$3\frac{5}{8} \times \frac{1}{1} = 3\frac{5}{8}$ Find the common denominator (8) and rename the fractions.

$+2\frac{1}{2} \times \frac{4}{4} = +2\frac{4}{8}$ Add the fractions.

$5\frac{9}{5} = 6\frac{1}{8}$ Add the whole numbers. Simplify and rename improper fractions.

Add. Write answers in simplest form.

	a	b	c	d
1.	$2\frac{1}{2}$ $+3\frac{2}{5}$	$1\frac{2}{3}$ $+6\frac{1}{5}$	$4\frac{2}{7}$ $+3\frac{3}{4}$	$5\frac{1}{4}$ $+2\frac{1}{5}$
2.	$8\frac{1}{6}$ $+1\frac{4}{7}$	$2\frac{5}{6}$ $+6\frac{3}{5}$	$7\frac{3}{8}$ $+3\frac{1}{3}$	$4\frac{2}{9}$ $+9\frac{1}{2}$
3.	$9\frac{5}{6}$ $+6\frac{5}{8}$	$4\frac{1}{7}$ $+10\frac{2}{3}$	$8\frac{1}{9}$ $+2\frac{6}{7}$	$7\frac{3}{10}$ $+1\frac{5}{6}$

Lesson 5.4 Adding Mixed Numbers

Add. Write answers in simplest form.

	a	b	c	d

1.

a. $3\frac{2}{5}$ $+2\frac{3}{10}$

b. $7\frac{3}{8}$ $+\ \frac{3}{4}$

c. $4\frac{1}{2}$ $+2\frac{2}{3}$

d. $5\frac{1}{2}$ $+\ \frac{5}{6}$

2.

a. $2\frac{3}{4}$ $+1\frac{1}{6}$

b. $2\frac{1}{2}$ $+3\frac{5}{8}$

c. $3\frac{2}{3}$ $+\ \frac{5}{6}$

d. $1\frac{1}{8}$ $+3\frac{3}{4}$

3.

a. $5\frac{7}{10}$ $+8\frac{2}{3}$

b. $11\frac{4}{5}$ $+2\frac{8}{9}$

c. $6\frac{7}{8}$ $+5\frac{1}{6}$

d. $9\frac{5}{7}$ $+9\frac{9}{10}$

4.

a. $1\frac{1}{2}$ $2\frac{1}{3}$ $+\ \frac{3}{4}$

b. $2\frac{3}{8}$ $3\frac{1}{4}$ $+2\frac{1}{2}$

c. $\frac{2}{3}$ $1\frac{1}{2}$ $+2\frac{1}{4}$

d. $2\frac{3}{8}$ $3\frac{1}{2}$ $+1\frac{1}{4}$

5.

a. $2\frac{1}{6}$ $3\frac{2}{3}$ $+1\frac{1}{2}$

b. $\frac{5}{6}$ $2\frac{1}{2}$ $+\ \frac{2}{3}$

c. $3\frac{5}{8}$ $2\frac{1}{4}$ $+2\frac{1}{2}$

d. $1\frac{2}{3}$ $3\frac{1}{2}$ $+1\frac{3}{5}$

Lesson 5.5 Subtracting Mixed Numbers

$6\frac{5}{7} \times \frac{3}{3} = 6\frac{15}{21}$ Rename fractions to have common denominators.

$-5\frac{1}{3} \times \frac{7}{7} = -5\frac{7}{21}$ Subtract the fractions, then subtract the whole numbers.

$1\frac{8}{21}$ Write the difference in simplest form.

Subtract. Write answers in simplest form.

	a	b	c	d	e
1.	$4\frac{2}{3}$ $-2\frac{1}{6}$	$7\frac{7}{8}$ $-2\frac{3}{4}$	$8\frac{9}{10}$ $-6\frac{2}{5}$	$8\frac{3}{4}$ $-4\frac{3}{8}$	$3\frac{1}{3}$ $-2\frac{2}{9}$
2.	$6\frac{5}{8}$ $-4\frac{3}{7}$	$5\frac{1}{2}$ $-1\frac{1}{6}$	$9\frac{7}{8}$ $-4\frac{2}{5}$	$9\frac{5}{9}$ $-3\frac{1}{3}$	$7\frac{7}{10}$ $-4\frac{4}{7}$
3.	$8\frac{8}{12}$ $-2\frac{3}{4}$	$9\frac{3}{10}$ $-6\frac{1}{8}$	$8\frac{4}{6}$ $-5\frac{2}{8}$	$6\frac{6}{7}$ $-3\frac{3}{5}$	$5\frac{5}{6}$ $-3\frac{1}{12}$

Lesson 5.5 Subtracting Mixed Numbers

Subtract. Write answers in simplest form.

	a	b	c	d

1.
$$4 \\ -\frac{3}{8}$$
$$5\frac{5}{6} \\ -1\frac{1}{3}$$
$$8 \\ -3\frac{5}{8}$$
$$4\frac{3}{5} \\ -\frac{3}{10}$$

2.
$$5\frac{3}{4} \\ -4\frac{5}{8}$$
$$8\frac{2}{3} \\ -4\frac{1}{6}$$
$$5\frac{5}{6} \\ -3\frac{3}{4}$$
$$7\frac{4}{5} \\ -2\frac{1}{2}$$

3.
$$5\frac{3}{8} \\ -2\frac{7}{8}$$
$$3\frac{1}{4} \\ -2\frac{3}{4}$$
$$8\frac{2}{5} \\ -3\frac{4}{5}$$
$$1\frac{1}{3} \\ -\frac{2}{3}$$

4.
$$4\frac{3}{4} \\ -2\frac{7}{8}$$
$$6\frac{1}{2} \\ -3\frac{2}{3}$$
$$5 \\ -2\frac{3}{3}$$
$$3 \\ -\frac{5}{6}$$

5.
$$2\frac{1}{2} \\ -1\frac{4}{11}$$
$$5\frac{7}{10} \\ -2\frac{3}{8}$$
$$9\frac{7}{8} \\ -8\frac{2}{9}$$
$$7\frac{3}{4} \\ -6\frac{7}{12}$$

Lesson 5.6 Problem Solving

SHOW YOUR WORK

Solve each problem. Write answers in simplest form.

1. Caroline needs $3\frac{1}{7}$ cups of sugar for her first batch of brownies and $2\frac{8}{9}$ cups of sugar for a second batch. How much sugar does she need in all?

   Caroline needs _____ cups of sugar.

2. Robert's gas tank has $5\frac{3}{5}$ gallons of gas in it. If he adds $7\frac{2}{3}$ gallons, how much gas will be in the tank?

   There will be _____ gallons of gas in the tank.

3. A hamburger weighs $\frac{1}{3}$ pound, and an order of french fries weighs $\frac{1}{4}$ pound. How many pounds total will a meal of hamburger and french fries weigh?

   The meal will weigh _____ pounds.

4. John is $5\frac{6}{10}$ feet tall and Jamar is $\frac{5}{8}$ feet taller than John. How tall is Jamar?

   Jamar is _____ feet tall.

5. Mrs. Stevenson has used $4\frac{2}{3}$ inches of string. She needs $1\frac{6}{7}$ inches more. How much string will Mrs. Stevenson have used when she is done?

   Mrs. Stevenson will have used _____ inches of string.

6. It takes Lacy $8\frac{1}{3}$ seconds to climb up the slide and $2\frac{1}{4}$ seconds to go down the slide. How many seconds is Lacy's trip up and down the slide?

   Lacy's trip is _____ seconds long.

1.	2.
3.	4.
5.	6.

Lesson 5.6 Problem Solving

Solve each problem. Write answers in simplest form.

1. Eric needs $\frac{1}{2}$ deck of playing cards for a magic trick. He only has $\frac{2}{7}$ of a deck. What fraction of a deck does Eric still need?

   Eric still needs _____ of a deck.

2. Randy ran $1\frac{3}{4}$ miles. Natasha ran $\frac{9}{10}$ miles. How many more miles did Randy run than Natasha?

   Randy ran _____ miles more than Natasha.

3. A soccer ball weighs 6 ounces when fully inflated. Raymundo has inflated the ball to $4\frac{2}{3}$ ounces. How many more ounces must be added before the ball is fully inflated?

   The ball needs _____ more ounces to be fully inflated.

4. In January, employees at Home Real Estate Company worked $6\frac{3}{4}$ hours a day. In February, employees worked $7\frac{1}{8}$ hours a day. How many more hours did employees work daily during February than during January?

   Employees worked _____ hours more during February.

5. Peter's hat size is $7\frac{3}{8}$ units. Cal's hat size is $6\frac{7}{12}$ units. How many units larger is Peter's hat size than Cals?

   Peter's hat size is _____ units larger than Cal's.

6. Mrs. Anderson uses $3\frac{1}{5}$ cups of apples for her pies. Mrs. Woods uses $4\frac{2}{3}$ cups of apples for her pies. How many more cups of apples does Mrs. Woods use than Mrs. Anderson?

   Mrs. Woods uses _____ more cups of apples.

1.	2.
3.	4.
5.	6.

Check What You Learned

Adding and Subtracting Fractions

Add or subtract. Write answers in simplest form.

	a	b	c	d

1.

a. $+\dfrac{4}{6}$ $\dfrac{1}{6}$

b. $+\dfrac{3}{7}$ $\dfrac{2}{7}$

c. $+\dfrac{2}{9}$ $\dfrac{6}{9}$

d. $+\dfrac{7}{8}$ $\dfrac{2}{8}$

2.

a. $+\dfrac{7}{12}$ $\dfrac{3}{5}$

b. $+\dfrac{2}{5}$ $\dfrac{9}{10}$

c. $5\dfrac{2}{5} + 7\dfrac{2}{3}$

d. $8\dfrac{3}{10} + 9\dfrac{2}{4}$

3.

a. $\dfrac{5}{9} - \dfrac{2}{9}$

b. $\dfrac{6}{7} - \dfrac{5}{7}$

c. $\dfrac{5}{8} - \dfrac{1}{4}$

d. $\dfrac{5}{6} - \dfrac{7}{12}$

4.

a. $4 - \dfrac{5}{6}$

b. $6\dfrac{2}{3} - 4\dfrac{1}{3}$

c. $5\dfrac{2}{7} - 4\dfrac{1}{4}$

d. $9\dfrac{1}{9} - 1\dfrac{4}{5}$

NAME _____

Check What You Learned

SHOW YOUR WORK

Adding and Subtracting Fractions

Solve each problem.

5. Lauren practiced tennis twice last week. On Tuesday, she practiced $2\frac{4}{8}$ hours. On Thursday, she practiced $1\frac{2}{6}$ hours. How much longer did Lauren practice on Tuesday?

   Lauren practiced _____ hours longer on Tuesday.

6. Mr. Daniels' chili recipe calls for 5 cups of diced tomatoes and $\frac{1}{4}$ cup of diced green chilies. How many cups of tomatoes and green chilies does Mr. Daniels need altogether?

   Mr. Daniels needs _____ cups of tomatoes and green chilies altogether.

7. Ben watched a baseball game for $2\frac{1}{5}$ hours. Drew watched a football game for $2\frac{2}{8}$ hours. How much time altogether did Ben and Drew spend watching the games?

   They spent _____ hours watching the games.

8. The Rizzo's farm has $9\frac{1}{2}$ acres of corn. The Johnson's farm has $7\frac{1}{3}$ acres of corn. How many more acres of corn does the Rizzo's farm have?

   The Rizzo's farm has _____ more acres of corn.

9. Jeremy cleans his house in $2\frac{1}{2}$ hours. Hunter cleans his house in $3\frac{1}{4}$ hours. How much longer does it take Hunter to clean a house than Jeremy?

   It takes Hunter _____ hours longer to clean his house.

5.

6.

7.

8.

9.

CHAPTER 5 POSTTEST

Mid-Test Chapters 1–5

Add, subtract, multiply, or divide

	a	b	c	d
1.	275 × 56	312 × 9	1717 × 34	5806 × 42
2.	8)‾72‾	19)‾384‾	52)‾6147‾	8)‾1352‾
3.	5.73 0.21 + 1.6	28.30 1.07 + 5.58	93.45 28.12 + 23.3	27.38 92.46 + 84.9
4.	42.5 − 16.30	7.28 − 0.95	74.27 − 2.56	32.56 − 23.65
5.	586 × 3.7	2.1 × 0.8	3.50 × 2.6	38.2 × 7.58

Mid-Test Chapters 1–5

Multiply or divide.

	a	b	c	d
6.	98 × 0.4	370 × 6.4	7.02 × 9	42.36 × 13

7.

a	b	c	d
2.5)‾10‾	0.03)‾36‾	9)‾7.2‾	8)‾5.6‾

8.

a	b	c	d
4.8)‾24.96‾	0.37)‾2.96‾	9.06)‾63.42‾	1.21)‾4.84‾

Write each number in expanded form.

	a	b	c
9.	732	32,132	4,790
	_____	_____	_____
10.	10.03	23,147.32	300.1
	_____	_____	_____

What is the value of the underlined digit?

11.	153<u>9</u>.16	8<u>9</u>8,792	3<u>5</u>,563.8
	_____	_____	_____
12.	<u>3</u>,324,291.4	8,524.1<u>4</u>	82,917.<u>2</u>
	_____	_____	_____

Mid-Test Chapters 1–5

Add or subtract. Write answers in simplest form.

	a	b	c	d
13.	$+\ \dfrac{3}{4}$ $\dfrac{1}{4}$	$+\ \dfrac{2}{7}$ $\dfrac{3}{5}$	$+\ \dfrac{7}{8}$ $\dfrac{1}{3}$	$+\ \dfrac{5}{\ }$ $\dfrac{2}{3}$
14.	$-\ \dfrac{5}{8}$ $\dfrac{1}{8}$	$-\ \dfrac{6}{9}$ $\dfrac{2}{3}$	$-\ \dfrac{10}{11}$ $\dfrac{4}{5}$	$-\ \dfrac{7}{\ }$ $\dfrac{3}{4}$
15.	$+\ 2\dfrac{3}{4}$ $4\dfrac{2}{3}$	$+\ 8\dfrac{1}{3}$ $8\dfrac{5}{7}$	$+\ 2\dfrac{5}{8}$ $9\dfrac{3}{4}$	$+\ 2\dfrac{5}{6}$ $1\dfrac{1}{8}$
16.	$-\ 5\dfrac{7}{12}$ $1\dfrac{5}{12}$	$-\ 7\dfrac{1}{4}$ $3\dfrac{2}{9}$	$-\ 8\dfrac{1}{4}$ $5\dfrac{3}{4}$	$-\ 8\dfrac{1}{3}$ $3\dfrac{1}{2}$

Simplify each of the following.

	a	b	c
17.	$\dfrac{18}{20}$ _____	$\dfrac{28}{35}$ _____	$2\dfrac{2}{12}$ _____
18.	$3\dfrac{4}{6}$ _____	$\dfrac{51}{6}$ _____	$7\dfrac{8}{12}$ _____

Mid-Test Chapters 1–5

Write each improper fraction as a mixed number in simplest form.

	a	b	c
19.	$\dfrac{18}{8}$ _____	$\dfrac{51}{9}$ _____	$\dfrac{34}{3}$ _____
20.	$\dfrac{53}{12}$ _____	$\dfrac{82}{8}$ _____	$\dfrac{66}{7}$ _____

Write each mixed number as an improper fraction.

	a	b	c
21.	$4\dfrac{1}{3}$ _____	$7\dfrac{5}{9}$ _____	$1\dfrac{7}{10}$ _____
22.	$3\dfrac{3}{4}$ _____	$5\dfrac{11}{12}$ _____	$8\dfrac{2}{9}$ _____

Compare each pair of numbers using <, >, or =.

	a	b	c	d
23.	$\dfrac{7}{8}$ ___ $\dfrac{9}{10}$	$\dfrac{1}{4}$ ___ $\dfrac{4}{10}$	$\dfrac{2}{3}$ ___ $\dfrac{9}{10}$	$\dfrac{8}{10}$ ___ $\dfrac{2}{3}$
24.	80.59 ___ 80.67	46.94 ___ 46.37	54.72 ___ 54.27	86.4 ___ 86.40

Put the numbers in order from least to greatest.

25. $0.1, \dfrac{1}{4}, 3.1, \dfrac{1}{3}$

_____

26. $0.5, \dfrac{5}{8}, 0.7, \dfrac{1}{9}$

_____

27. $\dfrac{3}{2}, 1.7, \dfrac{1}{150}, \dfrac{8}{3}$

_____

NAME _____

 Check What You Know

Multiplying and Dividing Fractions

Multiply. Write answers in simplest form.

	a	b	c
1.	$\frac{1}{2} \times \frac{1}{3} =$ ___	$\frac{3}{4} \times \frac{2}{7} =$ ___	$\frac{1}{4} \times \frac{4}{5} =$ ___
2.	$\frac{2}{5} \times \frac{5}{8} =$ ___	$\frac{4}{9} \times \frac{1}{2} =$ ___	$5 \times \frac{2}{7} =$ ___
3.	$3 \times \frac{4}{8} =$ ___	$\frac{4}{9} \times 7 =$ ___	$\frac{3}{4} \times 2 =$ ___
4.	$2\frac{3}{4} \times 2 =$ ___	$1\frac{3}{8} \times 3 =$ ___	$1\frac{1}{2} \times 2 =$ ___

Divide. Write answers in simplest form.

5.	$6 \div \frac{1}{10} =$ ___	$\frac{1}{8} \div 14 =$ ___	$1 \div \frac{1}{4} =$ ___
6.	$\frac{1}{9} \div 2 =$ ___	$\frac{1}{5} \div 6 =$ ___	$7 \div \frac{1}{4} =$ ___
7.	$\frac{1}{5} \div 4 =$ ___	$11 \div \frac{1}{8} =$ ___	$\frac{1}{9} \div 2 =$ ___
8.	$3 \div \frac{1}{5} =$ ___	$\frac{1}{3} \div 8 =$ ___	$6 \div \frac{1}{12} =$ ___

Check What You Know

SHOW YOUR WORK

Multiplying and Dividing Fractions

Solve each problem. Write answers in simplest form.

9. Aimee lives $\frac{8}{9}$ miles from the park. She has walked $\frac{3}{5}$ of the way to the park. How far has Aimee walked?

   Aimee has walked _____ miles.

   9.

10. Hotah and his 3 friends are each running $\frac{1}{4}$ of a 2-mile relay race. How far is each person running?

    Each person is running _____ miles.

    10.

11. A single serving of jello requires $\frac{1}{8}$ cups sugar. How much sugar is needed for 6 servings?

    _____ cups are needed.

    11.

12. Isabel watched a movie that was 4 hours long. She stood up every $\frac{1}{4}$ hour to stretch her legs. How many times did Isabel stand up during the movie?

    Isabel stood up _____ times during the movie.

    12.

13. Suppose 8 books are stacked on top of one another. Each book is $1\frac{5}{9}$ inches thick. How high is the stack of books?

    The stack of books is _____ inches high.

    13.

14. Beth has to carry 9 grocery bags into the house. Each grocery bag weighs $5\frac{3}{5}$ pounds. How many pounds does Beth carry in all?

    Beth carries _____ pounds.

    14.

Lesson 6.1 Multiplying Fractions Using Models

You can use visual models to multiply fractions.

$7 \times \frac{1}{2}$

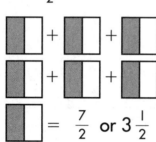

$= \frac{7}{2}$ or $3\frac{1}{2}$

or

Or, you can follow the mathematical procedure.

$$7 \times \frac{1}{2}$$

$$\frac{7}{1} \times \frac{1}{2}$$

$$\frac{7 \times 1}{1 \times 2} = \frac{7}{2} \text{ or } 3\frac{1}{2}$$

Use visual models to solve each problem. Write answers in simplest form.

	a	**b**	**c**
1.	$3 \times \frac{1}{8} =$ ___	$5 \times \frac{2}{3} =$ ___	$\frac{2}{9} \times 8 =$ ___

Multiply. Write answers in simplest form.

	a	**b**	**c**	**d**
2.	$\frac{8}{9} \times 4 =$ ___	$\frac{1}{8} \times 8 =$ ___	$\frac{4}{5} \times 6 =$ ___	$9 \times \frac{1}{3} =$ ___
3.	$5 \times \frac{3}{10} =$ ___	$\frac{2}{3} \times 3 =$ ___	$9 \times \frac{7}{8} =$ ___	$\frac{6}{11} \times 7 =$ ___

Lesson 6.2 Multiplying Fractions Using Rules

$$\frac{3}{4} \times \frac{1}{6} = \frac{3 \times 1}{4 \times 6}$$ ← - - - - - Multiply the numerators. - - - - - → $$\frac{2}{7} \times \frac{7}{10} = \frac{2 \times 7}{7 \times 10}$$

$$= \frac{3}{24}$$ ← - - - - Multiply the denominators. - - - - → $$= \frac{14}{70}$$

$$= \frac{1}{8}$$ ← - - - - - Reduce to simplest form. - - - - - → $$= \frac{1}{5}$$

Multiply. Write answers in simplest form.

	a	b	c
1.	$\frac{1}{3} \times \frac{2}{9} =$ ___	$\frac{1}{8} \times \frac{2}{5} =$ ___	$\frac{3}{7} \times \frac{3}{4} =$ ___
2.	$\frac{5}{6} \times \frac{3}{8} =$ ___	$\frac{5}{9} \times \frac{3}{7} =$ ___	$\frac{6}{11} \times \frac{1}{6} =$ ___
3.	$\frac{3}{5} \times \frac{2}{3} =$ ___	$\frac{3}{7} \times \frac{1}{3} =$ ___	$\frac{1}{6} \times \frac{8}{9} =$ ___
4.	$\frac{7}{10} \times \frac{4}{5} =$ ___	$\frac{7}{8} \times \frac{2}{7} =$ ___	$\frac{1}{2} \times \frac{5}{11} =$ ___
5.	$\frac{5}{7} \times \frac{7}{9} =$ ___	$\frac{3}{4} \times \frac{9}{10} =$ ___	$\frac{7}{12} \times \frac{7}{11} =$ ___

Lesson 6.3 Multiplying Mixed Numbers

$2\frac{1}{5} \times 1\frac{1}{4} = \frac{11}{5} \times \frac{5}{4}$ Rewrite the mixed numbers as improper fractions.

$= \frac{55}{20}$ Multiply the fractions.

$= 2\frac{15}{20} = 2\frac{3}{4}$ Write the answer in simplest form.

Multiply. Write answers in simplest form.

	a	b	c	d
1.	$2\frac{1}{4} \times 2\frac{1}{3} =$ ____	$5\frac{1}{2} \times 1\frac{1}{6} =$ ____	$3\frac{1}{4} \times 4\frac{2}{3} =$ ____	$1\frac{6}{7} \times 2\frac{2}{3} =$ ____
2.	$1\frac{7}{10} \times 4\frac{3}{4} =$ ____	$3\frac{3}{5} \times 4\frac{1}{7} =$ ____	$1\frac{5}{9} \times 3\frac{1}{2} =$ ____	$6\frac{2}{3} \times 2\frac{1}{9} =$ ____
3.	$5\frac{3}{5} \times 2\frac{1}{4} =$ ____	$6\frac{1}{3} \times 1\frac{2}{5} =$ ____	$9\frac{1}{2} \times 2\frac{2}{7} =$ ____	$2\frac{6}{7} \times 5\frac{1}{7} =$ ____
4.	$8\frac{1}{6} \times 2\frac{1}{2} =$ ____	$3\frac{1}{8} \times 1\frac{5}{8} =$ ____	$7\frac{1}{2} \times 1\frac{1}{5} =$ ____	$3\frac{5}{6} \times 3\frac{1}{5} =$ ____
5.	$1\frac{7}{12} \times 2\frac{5}{6} =$ ____	$2\frac{1}{6} \times 7\frac{1}{2} =$ ____	$2\frac{1}{8} \times 3\frac{1}{4} =$ ____	$8\frac{2}{3} \times 4\frac{1}{2} =$ ____

Lesson 6.4 Dividing Fractions by Whole Numbers Using Models

When dividing fractions, you are splitting one fraction into smaller pieces.

If 5 people evenly split $\frac{1}{3}$ of a pan of brownies, how much will each person receive?

$\frac{1}{3}$ pan of brownies

Divide the third into 5 pieces.

Each person receives $\frac{1}{15}$ of the original pan of brownies.

Use drawings to solve each problem.

	a	**b**
1.	$\frac{1}{4} \div 7 =$	$\frac{1}{3} \div 3 =$
2.	$\frac{1}{5} \div 9 =$	$\frac{1}{2} \div 6 =$
3.	$\frac{1}{2} \div 7 =$	$\frac{1}{6} \div 2 =$

Lesson 6.5 Dividing Fractions by Whole Numbers Using Rules

To divide a fraction by a whole number, first write the whole number as a fraction. Then, multiply by the reciprocal of the divisor.

divisor → reciprocal →

$$\frac{1}{5} \div 8 = \frac{1}{5} \div \frac{8}{1} = \frac{1}{5} \times \frac{1}{8}$$

$$= \frac{1 \times 1}{5 \times 8} \quad \text{Multiply across the numerators and denominators.}$$

$$= \frac{1}{40} \quad \text{Write the answer in simplest form.}$$

Divide. Write answers in simplest form.

	a	b	c	d
1.	$\frac{1}{3} \div 3 =$ ___	$\frac{1}{5} \div 8 =$ ___	$\frac{1}{6} \div 5 =$ ___	$\frac{1}{8} \div 3 =$ ___
2.	$\frac{1}{3} \div 12 =$ ___	$\frac{1}{7} \div 2 =$ ___	$\frac{1}{9} \div 10 =$ ___	$\frac{1}{6} \div 6 =$ ___
3.	$\frac{1}{4} \div 12 =$ ___	$\frac{1}{8} \div 5 =$ ___	$\frac{1}{8} \div 6 =$ ___	$\frac{1}{10} \div 4 =$ ___
4.	$\frac{1}{5} \div 12 =$ ___	$\frac{1}{7} \div 7 =$ ___	$\frac{1}{6} \div 8 =$ ___	$\frac{1}{12} \div 5 =$ ___

Lesson 6.6 Dividing Whole Numbers by Fractions

To divide a whole number by a fraction, first write the whole number as a fraction. Then, multiply by the reciprocal of the divisor.

$$6 \div \frac{1}{8} = \overset{\text{divisor}}{\frac{6}{1}} \times \overset{\text{reciprocal}}{\frac{8}{1}}$$

$$= \frac{6 \times 8}{1 \times 1}$$ Multiply across the numerators and denominators.

$$= \frac{48}{1} = 48$$ Write the answer in simplest form.

Divide. Write answers in simplest form.

	a	b	c	d
1.	$5 \div \frac{1}{3} = $ ___	$6 \div \frac{1}{8} = $ ___	$2 \div \frac{1}{5} = $ ___	$8 \div \frac{1}{7} = $ ___
2.	$9 \div \frac{1}{4} = $ ___	$10 \div \frac{1}{6} = $ ___	$15 \div \frac{1}{5} = $ ___	$4 \div \frac{1}{8} = $ ___
3.	$4 \div \frac{1}{5} = $ ___	$5 \div \frac{1}{9} = $ ___	$5 \div \frac{1}{5} = $ ___	$10 \div \frac{1}{11} = $ ___
4.	$4 \div \frac{1}{12} = $ ___	$6 \div \frac{1}{9} = $ ___	$3 \div \frac{1}{7} = $ ___	$5 \div \frac{1}{12} = $ ___

Lesson 6.6 Dividing Whole Numbers by Fractions

Divide. Write answers in simplest form.

	a	b	c	d
1.	$4 \div \frac{1}{3} =$ ___	$12 \div \frac{1}{5} =$ ___	$19 \div \frac{1}{6} =$ ___	$10 \div \frac{1}{6} =$ ___
2.	$17 \div \frac{1}{4} =$ ___	$16 \div \frac{1}{9} =$ ___	$9 \div \frac{1}{6} =$ ___	$7 \div \frac{1}{2} =$ ___
3.	$2 \div \frac{1}{5} =$ ___	$14 \div \frac{1}{5} =$ ___	$4 \div \frac{1}{10}$ ___	$8 \div \frac{1}{8} =$ ___
4.	$2 \div \frac{1}{7} =$ ___	$16 \div \frac{1}{5} =$ ___	$13 \div \frac{1}{5} =$ ___	$12 \div \frac{1}{3} =$ ___
5.	$5 \div \frac{1}{7} =$ ___	$3 \div \frac{1}{9} =$ ___	$15 \div \frac{1}{8} =$ ___	$6 \div \frac{1}{7} =$ ___
6.	$11 \div \frac{1}{2} =$ ___	$19 \div \frac{1}{3} =$ ___	$8 \div \frac{1}{9} =$ ___	$18 \div \frac{1}{5} =$ ___

Lesson 6.7 Problem Solving

Solve each problem. Write answers in simplest form.

1. Simon bought $\frac{2}{3}$ pounds of cookies. He ate $\frac{4}{5}$ of the cookies he bought. What was the weight of the cookies that Simon ate?

   Simon ate _____ pounds of cookies.

2. Students must take their tests home to be signed. Two-thirds of the class took home their tests. Only $\frac{1}{8}$ of the students who took their tests home got them signed. What fraction of the entire class got their tests signed?

   _____ of the class got their tests signed.

3. One serving of pancakes calls for $\frac{1}{3}$ cups of milk. How many cups of milk are needed for 4 servings of pancakes?

   _____ cups of milk are needed for four servings of pancakes.

4. If Carlos works $\frac{5}{12}$ of a day every day, how much will Carlos have worked after 5 days?

   After five days, Carlos worked _____ days.

5. Tony had $1\frac{1}{2}$ gallons of orange juice. He drank $\frac{2}{7}$ of the orange juice he had. How much orange juice did Tony drink?

   Tony drank _____ gallons of orange juice.

6. Miranda has 3 kites. Each kite needs $4\frac{2}{3}$ yards of string. How much string does Miranda need for all 3 kites?

   Miranda needs _____ yards of string.

1.	2.
3.	4.
5.	6.

Lesson 6.7 Problem Solving

Solve each problem. Write answers in simplest form.

1. Howard read $\frac{1}{16}$ of a book each day until he finished two books. How many days did it take Howard to read both books?

   Howard read his books for _____ days.

   1.

2. The school day is 7 hours long. If recess lasts $\frac{1}{4}$ hour, what fraction of the school day does recess make up?

   Recess is _____ of a school day.

   2.

3. Janet has 8 ounces of coffee beans. If each cup of coffee requires $\frac{1}{9}$ ounce of coffee beans, how many cups of coffee can Janet make?

   Janet can make _____ cups of coffee.

   3.

4. A recipe for one dozen cookies requires $\frac{1}{2}$ cup of flour. How much flour is needed for each cookie?

   Each cookie requires _____ cup of flour.

   4.

5. Keith has 7 yards of string. He needs $\frac{1}{3}$ yard of string for each of his puppets. How many puppets can Keith make with his string?

   Keith can make _____ puppets.

   5.

6. Mr. Garcia worked 4 hours on Wednesday. He took a quick break every $\frac{1}{2}$ hour. How many breaks did Mr. Garcia take?

   Mr. Garcia took _____ breaks on Wednesday.

   6.

Check What You Learned

Multiplying and Dividing Fractions

Multiply. Write answers in simplest form.

	a	b	c
1.	$\frac{1}{4} \times \frac{8}{9} =$ ___	$\frac{3}{5} \times \frac{5}{6} =$ ___	$\frac{5}{7} \times \frac{1}{2} =$ ___
2.	$\frac{11}{12} \times \frac{2}{3} =$ ___	$\frac{3}{7} \times \frac{4}{5} =$ ___	$\frac{3}{4} \times \frac{3}{8} =$ ___
3.	$3 \times \frac{5}{8} =$ ___	$\frac{1}{6} \times 4 =$ ___	$\frac{1}{3} \times 9 =$ ___
4.	$2\frac{7}{8} \times 2 =$ ___	$1\frac{7}{12} \times 9 =$ ___	$3\frac{3}{10} \times 8 =$ ___

Divide. Write answers in simplest form.

	a	b	c
5.	$6 \div \frac{1}{8} =$ ___	$\frac{1}{9} \div 4 =$ ___	$2 \div \frac{1}{10} =$ ___
6.	$\frac{1}{3} \div 10 =$ ___	$\frac{1}{5} \div 4 =$ ___	$2 \div \frac{1}{8} =$ ___
7.	$\frac{1}{5} \div 6 =$ ___	$5 \div \frac{1}{3} =$ ___	$\frac{1}{8} \div 3 =$ ___
8.	$\frac{1}{3} \div 7 =$ ___	$5 \div \frac{1}{10} =$ ___	$\frac{1}{7} \div 12 =$ ___

CHAPTER 6 POSTTEST

Check What You Learned

SHOW YOUR WORK

Multiplying and Dividing Fractions

Solve each problem. Write answers in simplest form.

9. Five new dresses have been sewn. Chelsea did $\frac{1}{7}$ of the total sewing. What fraction of each dress did Chelsea sew?

Chelsea sewed _____ of each dress.

9.

10. A group of friends ordered 2 pizzas. Each friend ate $\frac{1}{2}$ of a pizza. What fraction of the 2 total pizzas did each friend eat?

Each friend ate _____ of the total pizza.

10.

11. A race track was $\frac{1}{4}$ mile long. If Martha ran around the race track $5\frac{1}{9}$ times, how many miles did Martha run?

Martha ran _____ miles.

11.

12. Andrew cut a rope $\frac{1}{7}$ of a yard long into 8 equal pieces. How long will each piece of rope be?

Each piece of rope will be _____ yard long.

12.

13. Roberto studied $1\frac{2}{5}$ hour every day for 7 days. How many hours did Roberto study in 7 days?

Roberto studied _____ hours.

13.

14. Ms. Perez bought $\frac{1}{3}$ pound of seed for 14 gardens. If each garden gets an equal amount of seed, how much seed will be in each garden?

Each garden will have _____ pound of seed.

14.

Check What You Know

Understanding Mathematical Equations

The table provides x coordinates. Complete the table with 2 sets of y coordinates.
Then, complete the graph based on the table.

1.

	Add 2	Add 3
1		
2		
3		
4		
5		
6		

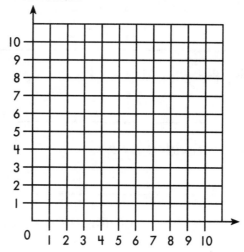

Find the value of each expression.

        a   **b**

2. $(8 + 2) \times 3 =$ _____ $(5 \div 3) + (6 \times 2) =$ _____

3. $[(3 \times 2) - 1] - 2 =$ _____ $\{[5 \times (1 + 1) + 5] - 6\} \times 2 =$ _____

4. $[(6 \times 4) - 4] \div 4 =$ _____ $(2 \times 3) + (5 \times 2) =$ _____

5. $5 + 2 \times 45 =$ _____ $88 - 7 \times 8 =$ _____

6. $98 + (5 \times 4) \div 2 =$ _____ $(9 - 6) \times 8 =$ _____

7. $43 + (9 \times 2) =$ _____ $66 \div (22 - 11) =$ _____

Check What You Know

Understanding Mathematical Equations

Write the expression for each phrase.

8. six more than the product of 2 and 3

_____

9. eight divided by the sum of 3 and 1

_____

10. four more than 25 divided by 5

_____

11. the difference between 21 and the product of 3 and 4

_____

SHOW YOUR WORK

Write the expression needed and solve each problem.

12. Rachel bought a sandwich for $3.95, a bag of chips for $1.50, and a drink for $1.25. The tax was $0.47. She gave the cashier $10.00. How much change should Rachel receive?

Expression: _____

Rachel should receive _____ in change.

12.

13. Ms. Garcia bought 3 packs of red notepads, 5 packs of yellow notepads, and 8 packs of green notepads. There were 3 notepads in each package. How many notepads did Ms. Garcia buy in all?

Expression: _____

Ms. Garcia bought _____ notepads.

13.

Lesson 7.1 Identifying and Graphing Number Patterns

Complete the table. Then, complete the graph based on the table.

	Add 1	Add 2
1	2	3
2	3	4
3	4	5
4	5	6
5	6	7
6	7	8

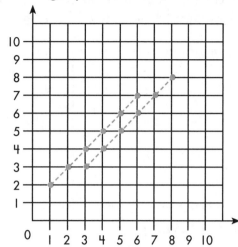

Complete each table and corresponding graph.

1.

a

	Add 2	Add 4
21		
22		
23		
24		
25		
26		

b

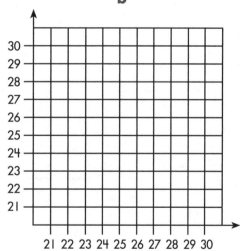

2.

	Add 1	Add 3
51		
52		
53		
54		
55		
56		

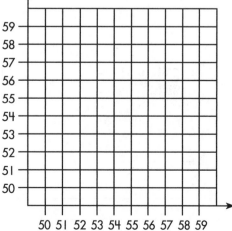

Lesson 7.2 Using Parentheses and Brackets

Parentheses, brackets, and braces can be used to show that one part of a mathematical expression should be solved before the rest of the equation.

Calculate the numbers in parentheses first.

$2 \times (3 \times 15) =$

$\qquad 2 \times 45 = 90$

When a problem has a combination of parentheses, brackets, and braces, work the problem from the inside out.

$[(3 \times 5) + 2] + 6 =$

$\qquad [15 + 2] + 6 =$

$\qquad\qquad 17 + 6 = 23$

Find the value of each expression.

$\qquad$ **a** $\qquad\qquad\qquad\qquad\qquad\qquad$ **b**

1. $(7 \times 5) \times 2 =$ _____ $\qquad (135 + 30) + 17$ _____

2. $(190 + 70) + 30 =$ _____ $\qquad [(11 \times 7) \times 5] \times 6 =$ _____

3. $\{[5 \times (6 - 1)] + 23\} + 17 =$ _____ $\quad [25 \times (8 + 2)] \times 2 =$ _____

4. $(1245 + 132) + 50 =$ _____ $\qquad (130 \times 3) \times 5 =$ _____

5. $\{70 + [5 \times (2 + 2)]\} + 35 =$ _____ $\quad [4 \times (3 \times 5)] \times 93$ _____

6. $(25 + 17) + 3 =$ _____ $\qquad 175 + \{32 + [(3 + 4) \times 2]\} =$ _____

Lesson 7.4 Simple Expressions

Key words can be used to figure out how to solve written expressions.

5 **more than** 3 **times** the **sum of** 4 and 2 $5 + [3 \times (4 + 2)]$

Write the expression for each phrase.

1. 2 less than 5   _____

2. 3 times the sum of 4 and 12   _____

3. 10 more than the quotient of 15 and 3   _____

4. 2 increased by 6 times 4   _____

5. $\frac{2}{3}$ of 30 minus 11   _____

6. Twice the difference between 8 and 2   _____

7. 6 times 4 plus 3 times 4   _____

8. $\frac{1}{4}$ times 8 increased by 11   _____

Lesson 7.4 Simple Expressions

Use each expression to write simple word problems.

1. $3 \times (2 + 8)$ _____

2. $6 \times (2 - \frac{1}{6})$ _____

3. $5 \times (3 + 5)$ _____

4. $20 \div (3 + 1)$ _____

5. $\frac{1}{4} \times 8 + 11$ _____

6. $12 \times (3 + 5)$ _____

7. $(8 + 4) \div 2$ _____

8. $9 \times 4 + 7$ _____

Lesson 7.5 Problem Solving

Key words in word problems can be used to create expressions to help solve the problems.

> how many more — subtraction
> total — addition
> of — multiplication
> split — division

SHOW YOUR WORK

List the key words in each word problem and name the operation they indicate. Then, solve.

1. Carmen wants to ride The Whirler, the roller coaster, and the log ride. The Whirler costs 3 tickets, the roller coaster costs 6 tickets, and the log ride costs 4 ticket. Carmen has 5 tickets. How many more tickets should Carmen buy?

   Carmen should buy _____ more tickets.

   1.

2. The high school has basketball, football, and track teams. There are 15 students on the basketball team and twice that number on the football team. There are 23 boys and 13 girls on the track team. If each student only participates in one group, how many students total are there on the basketball, football, and track teams?

   There are _____ students on the teams.

   2.

3. Nina always takes the same route when she walks her dog. First, she walks 5 blocks to the park. Then, she walks 6 blocks to the school. Finally, she walks 9 blocks home. Nina walks her dog 2 times each day. How many total blocks does Nina's dog walk each day?

   Nina's dog walks _____ blocks each day.

   3.

4. Julie bought 8 packages of cat food and 3 packages of dog food. Each package of cat food contained 5 cans. Each package of dog food contained 4 cans. How many more cans of cat food than dog food did Julie buy?

   Julie bought _____ more cans of cat food.

   4.

Lesson 7.5 Problem Solving

SHOW YOUR WORK

Write the expression needed and solve each problem.

1. Donnell had 15 stickers. He bought 30 stickers from a store in the mall and got 18 stickers for his birthday. Then, Donnell gave 6 of his stickers to his friend Tiger and used 8 to decorate a greeting card. How many stickers does Donnell have left?

    Donnell has _____ stickers left.

2. Brandt wants to ride the bumper cars 3 times and the zipper 5 times. It costs 2 tickets to ride the bumper cars and 4 tickets to ride the zipper. How many tickets does Brandt need?

    Brandt needs _____ tickets.

3. Briana is in a hiking club. The hiking club went on a hike to see a waterfall. To get to the hike the club members took 5 cars and 6 vans. There were 4 people in each car and 9 people in each van. How many people went on the hike?

    _____ people went on the hike.

4. Andy saved $32 in June, $27 in July, and $38 in August. Then Andy spent $18 on school supplies and $47 on new clothes. How much money does Andy have left?

    Andy has _____ left.

1.

2.

3.

4.

Check What You Learned

Understanding Mathematical Expressions

The table provides x coordinates. Complete the table with 2 sets of y coordinates. Then, complete the graph based on the table.

1.

	Add 4	Add 2
14		
15		
16		
17		
18		
19		

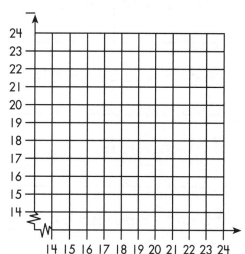

Find the value of each expression.

2. $(6 - 1) \times 3 =$ _____ $(9 + 5) - (3 \times 2) =$ _____

3. $[(4 \times 3) - 1] - 4 =$ _____ $\{[6 \times (1 + 2) + 4] - 5\} \times 3 =$ _____

4. $[(9 \times 5) - 3] \div 6 =$ _____ $(7 \times 4) + (8 \times 2) =$ _____

5. $(7 - 1) \times 4 =$ _____ $88 - 25 + 5 =$ _____

6. $[76 + (3 \times 3)] \div 5 =$ _____ $3 \times (1 + 9) =$ _____

7. $22 - (2 \times 9) =$ _____ $18 \div (6 - 3) =$ _____

Check What You Learned

Understanding Mathematical Expressions

Write the expression for each phrase.

8. eleven times the sum of 8 and 5

_____

9. six times the difference between 16 and 2

_____

10. one half of 8 increased by 6

_____

11. the sum of 8 and 12 divided by 4

_____

SHOW YOUR WORK

Write the expression needed and solve each problem.

12. Maria paints pictures and sells them at a gift shop. She charges $62.00 for a large painting and $25.50 for a small painting. Last month she sold eight large paintings and four small paintings. How much did she make in all?

Expression: _____

Maria made _____ in all.

12.

13. Brandon and Cole were playing touch football against Austin and Greg. Touchdowns were worth 7 points. Brandon and Cole scored 4 touchdowns. Austin and Greg's team scored 8 touchdowns. How many more points did Austin and Greg have than Brandon and Cole?

Expression: _____

They scored _____ more points.

13.

Check What You Know

Measurement Concepts

Complete the following.

	a	b
1.	6 ft. = _____ yd.	3 mi. = _____ ft.
2.	4 qt. = _____ pt.	2 mi. 3,400 ft. = _____ ft.
3.	5 gal. = _____ qt.	3 lb. = _____ oz.
4.	500 mm = _____ cm	6 L = _____ mL
5.	8 kg = _____ g	12,000 mL = _____ L

Draw a line plot to organize the data. Then, solve the problem.

6. Joseph needs to run 3 miles during his workout for the soccer team. He begins practice by running $\frac{1}{2}$ mile and he takes 3 breaks during practice to run $\frac{1}{4}$ mile each time. How much more will he need to run at the end of practice to finish his 3 miles?

Find the perimeter and area of the shapes below.

a

7.

4 ft.

6 ft.

P = _____

A = _____

b

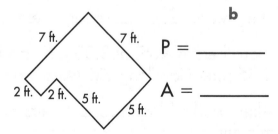

7 ft. 7 ft.

2 ft. 2 ft. 5 ft.

5 ft.

P = _____

A = _____

NAME _____

Check What You Know

Measurement Concepts

Find the volume of each rectangular solid.

        a   **b**

8. 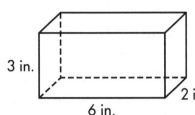   V = _____   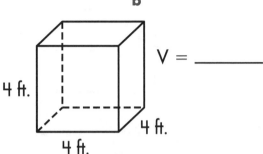   V = _____

SHOW YOUR WORK

Solve each problem.

9. Mr. Woodson built a rectangular fence around his yard. The fence is 60 feet long and 35 feet wide. What is the area of the yard?

The area of the yard is _____ square feet.

9.

10. Angelica is wrapping a present in a rectangular box. The box is 10 cm in height, 45 cm in length, and 20 cm in width. What is the volume of the box?

The volume of the box is _____ cubic centimeters.

10.

11. The school is standing students side-by-side to form a rectangle. If the rectangle is 20 meters long and 10 meters wide, what is its area?

The area is _____ square meters.

11.

12. Akira began work at 8:03 a.m. He finished at 4:35 p.m. How long did Akira work?

Akira worked for _____ hours and _____ minutes.

12.

Lesson 8.1 Metric Conversions

Length	Weight	Volume
1 kilometer (k) = 1,000 meters (m)	1 kilogram (kg) = 1,000 grams (g)	1 kiloliter (kL) = 1,000 liters (L)
1 meter (m) = 0.001 kilometers (km)	1 gram (g) = 0.001 kilograms (kg)	1 liter (L) = 0.001 kiloliters (kL)
1 meter (m) = 100 centimeters (cm)	1 gram (g) = 100 centigrams (cg)	1 liter = 100 centiliters (cL)
1 centimeter (cm) = 0.01 meters (m)	1 centigram (cg) = 0.01 grams (g)	1 centiliter (cL) = 0.01 liters (L)
1 meter (m) = 1,000 millimeters (mm)	1 gram (g) = 1,000 milligrams (mg)	1 liter (L) = 1,000 milliliters (mL)
1 millimeter (mm) = 0.001 meter (m)	1 milligram (mg) = 0.001 gram (g)	1 milliliter (mL) = 0.001 liters (L)

3 m = _____ cm	6 g = _____ mg	4 kL = _____ L
1 m = 100 cm	1 g = 1,000 mg	1 kL = 1,000 L
3 m = (3 × 100) cm	6 g = (6 × 1,000) mg	4 kL = (4 × 1,000) L
3 m = 300 cm	6 g = 6,000 mg	4 kL = 4,000 L

Complete the following.

	a	**b**
1.	5 g = _____ mg	17,000,000 mg = _____ kg
2.	4,000 L = _____ kL	51,000 mL = _____ L
3.	600 mm = _____ cm	8 m = _____ mm
4.	4 kL = _____ mL	46,000 L = _____ kL
5.	42 m = _____ mm	12 km = _____ m
6.	2 g 150 mg = _____ mg	4 kg 200 g = _____ g

SHOW YOUR WORK

7. Duane has a pencil 7 centimeters long. Fred has a pencil 64 millimeters long. Whose pencil is longer, and how much longer is it?

_____ pencil is _____ millimeters longer.

7.

8. Pedro has a stack of coins that weighs 85 grams. Conner has a stack of coins that weighs 64,300 milligrams. Whose stack of coins weighs more? How much more?

_____ stack of coins weighs _____ milligrams more.

8.

Lesson 8.2 Standard Measurement Conversions

Length	Weight	Volume
1 mile (mi.) = 1,760 yards (yd.)	1 gallon (gal.) = 4 quarts (qt.)	
1 mile (mi.) = 5,280 feet (ft.)	1 gallon (gal.) = 8 pints (pt.)	1 pound (lb.) = 16 ounces (oz.)
1 yard (yd.) = 36 inches (in.)	1 quart (qt.) = 2 pints (pt.)	
1 yard (yd.) = 3 feet (ft.)	1 quart (qt.) = 4 cups (c.)	2,000 pounds (lb.) = 1 ton (T.)
1 foot (ft.) = 12 inches (in.)	1 pint (pt.) = 2 cups (c.)	

Complete the following.

	a	b
1.	12 ft. = _____ yd.	120 in. = _____ ft.
2.	10 pt. = _____ qt.	9 pt. = _____ c.
3.	80 oz. = _____ lb.	1 T. = _____ oz.
4.	7 qt. = _____ c.	2 gal. = _____ pt.
5.	14,000 lb. = _____ T.	8 lb. = _____ oz.
6.	8 ft. 2 in. = _____ in.	18 ft. = _____ yd.
7.	1 T. 5 oz. = _____ oz.	144 oz. = _____ lb.
8.	8 gal. = _____ pt.	2 gal. 8 pt. = _____ pt.
9.	7 yd. = _____ in.	1 yd. 72 in. = _____ yd.
10.	5 qt. = _____ c.	2 qt. 3 c. = _____ c.
11.	2 mi. 3,241 ft. = _____ ft.	3 yd. 1 ft. = _____ ft.
12.	12 lb. 5 oz. = _____ oz.	10 T. 1,344 lb. = _____ lb.
13.	3 yd. = _____ ft.	3 qt. = _____ pt.
14.	1 gal. = _____ c.	1 lb. 5 oz. = _____ oz.
15.	28,000 lb. = _____ T.	3 pt. 6 c. = _____ c.
16.	9 qt. 4 pt. = _____ qt.	1 mi. 4 yd. = _____ yd.

Lesson 8.3 Using Line Plots to Solve Measurement Problems

A **line plot** is used to mark how many times something occurs in a data set. Line plots can be used to organize information to solve problems.

A pitcher holds 2 quarts of iced tea. There are several glasses being filled that hold various amounts—2 glasses hold $\frac{1}{8}$ qt., 1 glass holds $\frac{1}{4}$ qt., and 3 glasses hold $\frac{1}{3}$ qt. How much iced tea will be left in the pitcher?

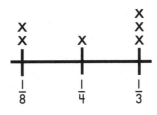

$$2 - [(2 \times \tfrac{1}{8}) + (\tfrac{1}{4}) + (3 \times \tfrac{1}{3})] =$$
$$2 - [(\tfrac{2}{8} + \tfrac{1}{4} + \tfrac{3}{3}) = 2 - (\tfrac{1}{4} + \tfrac{1}{4} + 1) =$$
$$2 - 1\tfrac{1}{2} = \tfrac{1}{2} \text{ qt.}$$

Draw a line plot to organize the information. Then, solve the problems.

1. Andre needs to get something out of the top of a closet, but cannot reach the shelf. He needs to construct something to stand on to reach the top, which is 3 feet too tall. He has 2 phone books that are each $\frac{1}{4}$ foot tall, 1 step stool that is $\frac{1}{2}$ foot tall, and one chair that is $1\frac{1}{3}$ feet tall. Will Andre's tower make him tall enough to reach the top?

2. Getting ready for a science experiment, Mr. Yip has put water into 8 1-pint beakers. Two beakers hold $\frac{1}{4}$ pint, 3 beakers hold $\frac{3}{8}$ pint, 2 beakers hold $\frac{5}{6}$ pint, and 1 beaker holds $\frac{5}{8}$ pint. If Mr. Yip wants to split the water equally between the 8 beakers, how much water will be in each beaker?

Lesson 8.4 Calculating Perimeter

The **perimeter** is the sum of the sides of a figure.

6 in. square diagram		

6 in. (top), 5 in. (right), 6 in. (bottom), in. (left)

$$\begin{array}{r} 6 \\ 5 \\ 6 \\ + \; 5 \\ \hline 22 \end{array}$$ or

$$6 \times 2 = 12$$
$$5 \times 2 = 10$$

$$\begin{array}{r} 12 \\ + \; 10 \\ \hline 22 \end{array}$$

To find the perimeter, add the length of the sides.

The perimeter of the rectangle is <u>22</u> in.

Find the perimeter of each figure.

a	**b**	**c**

1.

6 in. (top), 4 in. (left), 4 in. (right), 6 in. (bottom)

P = _____ in.

7 yd., 7 yd., 5 yd.

P = _____ yd.

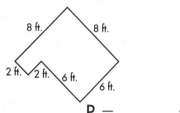
8 ft., 8 ft., 2 ft., 2 ft., 6 ft., 6 ft.

P = _____ ft.

2.

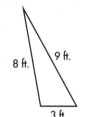
8 ft., 9 ft., 3 ft.

P = _____ ft.

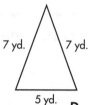
4 in., 4 in., 4 in., 4 in., 4 in., 4 in., 4 in., 4 in.

P = _____ in.

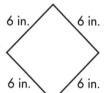
6 in., 6 in., 6 in., 6 in.

P = _____ in.

3.

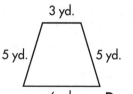
3 yd., 5 yd., 5 yd., 6 yd.

P = _____ yd.

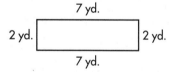
7 yd., 2 yd., 2 yd., 7 yd.

P = _____ yd.

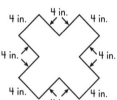
5 yd., 3 yd., 4 yd.

P = _____ yd.

4.

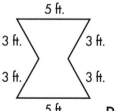
5 ft., 3 ft., 3 ft., 3 ft., 3 ft., 5 ft.

P = _____ ft.

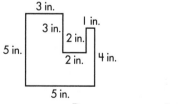
3 in., 3 in., 1 in., 2 in., 5 in., 2 in., 4 in., 5 in.

P = _____ in.

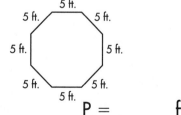
5 ft., 5 ft., 5 ft., 5 ft., 5 ft., 5 ft., 5 ft., 5 ft.

P = _____ ft.

Lesson 8.4 Calculating Perimeter

Find the perimeter of each figure.

a	b	c

1.

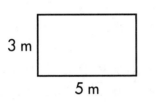
3 m
5 m

P = _____ m

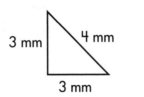
3 mm   4 mm
3 mm

P = _____ mm

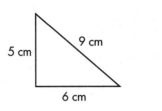
5 cm   9 cm
6 cm

P = _____ cm

2.

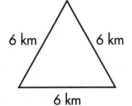
6 km   6 km
6 km

P = _____ km

7 cm
6 cm

P = _____ cm

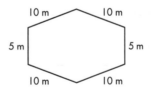
7 m   6 m
8 m

P = _____ m

3.

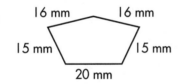
16 mm   16 mm
15 mm   15 mm
20 mm

P = _____ mm

10 m   10 m
5 m   5 m
10 m   10 m

P = _____ m

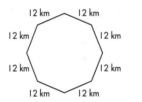
12 km   12 km
12 km   12 km
12 km   12 km
12 km   12 km

P = _____ km

4.

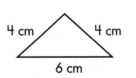
4 cm   4 cm
6 cm

P = _____ cm

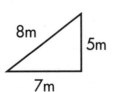
8m   5m
7m

P = _____ m

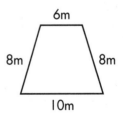
6m
8m   8m
10m

P = _____ m

Lesson 8.5 Calculating Area

Area is the number of square units needed to cover a surface.

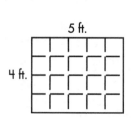

Length: 5 ft.
Width: 4 ft.

$$\begin{array}{r} 5 \text{ ft.} \\ \times\ 4 \text{ ft.} \\ \hline 20 \text{ square feet} \end{array}$$

To calculate the area of a square or rectangle, multiply the measure of the length by the measure of the width.

The area of a rectangle 5 feet in length and 4 feet in width is <u>20 square feet</u>.

Find the area of each figure.

	a	**b**	**c**

1.

5 in.

3 in.

A = ____ sq. in.

4 ft.

4 ft.

A = ____ sq. ft.

8 ft.

2 ft.

A = ____ sq. ft.

2.

7 yd.

2 yd.

A = ____ sq. yd.

7 in.

7 in.

A = ____ sq. in.

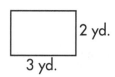

2 yd.

3 yd.

A = ____ sq. yd.

3.

8 ft.

8 ft.

A = ____ sq. ft.

9 in.

5 in.

A = ____ sq. in.

3 yd.

10 yd.

A = ____ sq. yd.

Lesson 8.5 Calculating Area

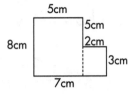

To calculate the area of an irregular shape, you must first divide the shape into smaller rectangles or squares.

$$\begin{array}{r} 8 \\ \times\ 5 \\ \hline 40 \end{array} \text{sq. cm}$$ $$\begin{array}{r} 2 \\ \times\ 3 \\ \hline 6 \end{array} \text{sq. cm}$$

Next, you must find the area of each individual rectangle or square.

$$\begin{array}{r} 40 \\ +\ 6 \\ \hline 46 \end{array} \text{sq. cm}$$

Then, add the area of each rectangle and square together to find the total area of the irregular shape.

The area of this shape is 46 square centimeters.

Find the area of each figure.

    a   **b**   **c**

1.

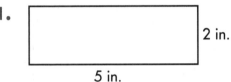

A = _____ sq. in.

7 in. / 9 in.

A = _____ sq. in.

3 in. / 3 in.

A = _____ sq. in.

2.

8 cm / 5 cm

A = _____ sq. cm

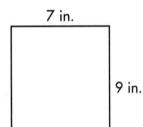

8 cm / 2 cm

A = _____ sq. cm

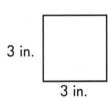

6 cm / 4 cm

A = _____ sq. cm

3.

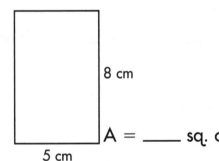

9 cm / 3 cm / 3 cm / 6 cm

A = _____ sq. cm

5 in. / 1 in. / 3 in. / 1 in.

A = _____ sq. in.

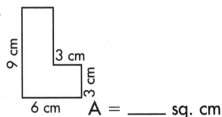

5 cm

A = _____ sq. cm

NAME _____

Models of Volume

The **volume** of a rectangular solid can be found by figuring out how many cubes of a particular unit size will fit inside the shape.

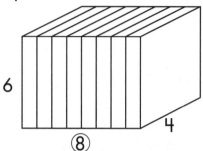

6   4   ⑧

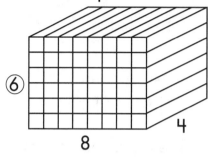

⑥   4   8

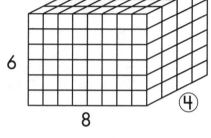

6   ④   8

First, divide the figure into given length units.

Next, divide the figure into given height units.

Last, divide the figure into given width units.

8   ×   6   ×   4 = 192 cubic units

Use the figures to find out how many units are in each figure.

1.

3   3   3

____ × ____ × ____ = ____ cubic units

2.

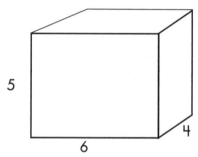

5   6   4

____ × ____ × ____ = ____ cubic units

3.

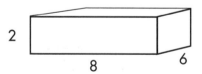

2   8   6

____ × ____ × ____ = ____ cubic units

4.

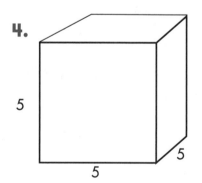

5   5   5

____ × ____ × ____ = ____ cubic units

Lesson 8.7 Calculating Volume

Volume is the number of cubic units needed to fill a given solid.

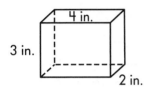

Length: 4 in.   Volume = length × width × height
Width: 2 in.   Volume = (4 in.) × (2 in.) × (3 in.)
Height: 3 in.

Volume = <u>24</u> cubic inches

Find the volume of each rectangular solid.

| a | b | c |

1.

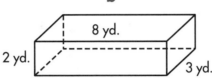

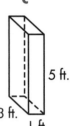

V = ____ cu. in.   V = ____ cu. yd.   V = ____ cu. ft.

2.

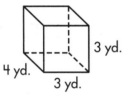

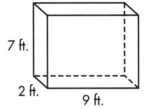

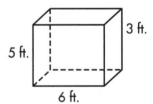

V = ____ cu. yd.   V = ____ cu. ft.   V = ____ cu. ft.

3.

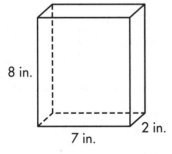

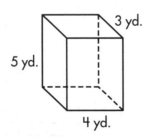

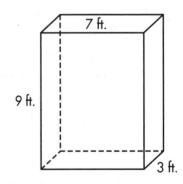

V = ____ cu. in.   V = ____ cu. yd.   V = ____ cu. ft.

Lesson 8.7 Calculating Volume

Find the volume of each rectangluar solid.

| a | b | c |

1.

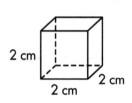

V = _____ cu. cm

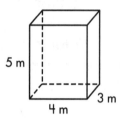

V = _____ cu. m

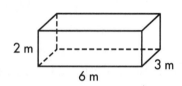

V = _____ cu. m

2.

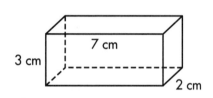

V = _____ cu. cm

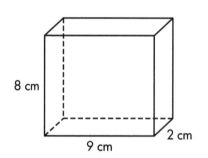

V = _____ cu. cm

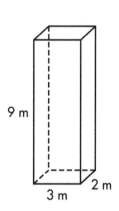

V = _____ cu. m

3.

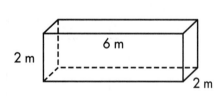

V = _____ cu. m

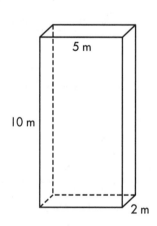

V = _____ cu. m

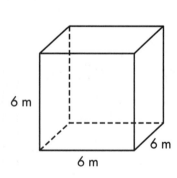

V = _____ cu. m

Lesson 8.7 Calculating Volume

Use the dimensions given to find the volume of the figures.

a   **b**

1.   Length = 12 centimeters   Length = 4 centimeters
     Width = 4 centimeters   Width = 11 centimeters
     Height = 6 centimeters   Height = 6 centimeters

     V = _____ cu. cm   V = _____ cu. cm

2.   Length = 4 meters   Length = 2 inches
     Width = 10 meters   Width = 6 inches
     Height = 5 meters   Height = 4 inches

     V = _____ cu. m   V = _____ cu. in.

3.   Length = 3 feet   Length = 12 inches
     Width = 2 feet   Width = 8 inches
     Height = 6 feet   Height = 4 inches

     V = _____ cu. ft.   V = _____ cu. in.

4.   Length = 10 inches   Length = 6 inches
     Width = 6 inches   Width = 9 inches
     Height = 2 inches   Height = 5 inches

     V = _____ cu. in.   V = _____ cu. in.

5.   Length = 8 inches   Length = 12 meters
     Width = 5 inches   Width = 8 meters
     Height = 3 inches   Height = 3 meters

     V = _____ cu. in.   V = _____ cu. m

Lesson 8.8 Problem Solving

Solve each problem.

1. Mr. Peate is building a rectangular fence around his house. The fence will be 32 feet long and 29 feet wide. What will be the perimeter of the fence?

   The perimeter will be _____ feet.

   1.

2. Sherman developed a photo 4 inches wide by 6 inches long. What is the area of the photograph?

   The photo is _____ square inches.

   2.

3. The Williams family bought a house 4,560 square feet in area. The house is 60 feet long. How wide is the house?

   The house is _____ feet wide.

   3.

4. Ms. Ferris owns a barn 12 yards long, 9 yards high, and 11 yards wide. If Ms. Ferris' barn is rectangular, what is the volume of her barn?

   The volume of her barn is _____ cubic yards.

   4.

5. The storage center sells rectangular storage spaces that are each 200 cubic feet. Each space is 5 feet long and 5 feet wide. What is the height of each storage space?

   Each storage space is _____ feet high.

   5.

6. A toy doll was sent to Lucy in a box 8 inches long, 5 inches wide, and 15 inches high. What is the volume of the box?

   The volume of the box is _____ cubic inches.

   6.

Lesson 8.8 Problem Solving

SHOW YOUR WORK

Solve each problem.

1. A soccer field is a rectangle. If a soccer field is 90 meters long and 45 meters wide, what is the perimeter of the soccer field?

   The perimeter of the field is _____ meters.

2. Julie is cutting out triangle pieces for her scrapbook. The sides of the triangle are 3 centimeters by 4 centimeters by 2 centimeters. What is the perimeter of the triangle?

   The perimeter of the triangle is _____ centimeters.

3. A rectangular town is 4 kilometers wide and 3 kilometers long. How many kilometers is it around the town?

   The perimeter is _____ kilometers.

4. Ian must mow a lawn 15 meters long and 9 meters wide. What is the area that Ian must mow?

   Ian must mow an area of _____ square meters.

5. Lea wants to put carpet on her bedroom floor. Her bedroom is 4 meters long and 6 meters wide. How much carpet does Lea need to cover the floor?

   Lea needs _____ square meters of carpet.

6. A swimming pool is 3 meters in depth, 8 meters in length, and 6 meters in width. What is the volume of the swimming pool?

   The volume of the swimming pool is _____ cubic meters.

1.

2.

3.

4.

5.

6.

Lesson 8.9 Elapsed Time

To calculate the amount of time that has elapsed, follow these steps:
1. Count the number of whole hours between the starting time and finishing time.
2. Count the remaining minutes.
3. Add the hours and minutes.

For example: start time: 9:39 a.m.
finish time: 4:16 p.m.

From 9:39 a.m. to 3:39 p.m., count 6 hours.
From 3:39 p.m. to 4:16 p.m., count 37 minutes.
The total time elapsed is 6 hours and 37 minutes.

Determine how much time has elapsed in each problem.

a   **b**

1.

Time elapsed:

_____ hours _____ minutes

Time elapsed:

_____ hours _____ minutes

2.

Arrival:	6:12 p.m.
Departure:	1:17 a.m.

Time elapsed:

_____ hours _____ minutes

Departure:	2:57 p.m.
Arrival:	9:21 p.m.

Time elapsed:

_____ hours _____ minutes

3.

Time start: _____ a.m.
Time finish: _____ a.m.
Time elapsed: _____

Time start: _____ a.m.
Time finish: _____ a.m.
Time elapsed: _____

Check What You Learned

Measurement Concepts

Complete the following.

	a	**b**
1.	9 yd. = _____ ft.	7 ft. 9 in. = _____ in.
2.	17 pt. = _____ c.	8 gal. 2 qt. = _____ qt.
3.	12 lb. = _____ oz.	14 T. = _____ lb.
4.	16 km = _____ m	6 m 36 cm = _____ cm
5.	7 kL = _____ mL	8 g 942 mg = _____ mg

Draw a line plot to organize the data and solve the problem.

6. Joanna needs 4 cups of milk to make pudding. She has $\frac{3}{4}$ cup of milk at home. She goes to borrow milk from her neighbors. One neighbor has $\frac{3}{4}$ cup, and two other neighbors give her $\frac{1}{2}$ cup. How much more milk will she need?

Find the perimeter and area of the shapes below.

a	**b**	**c**

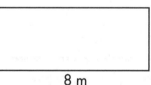

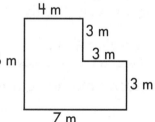

7.

P = _____   P = _____   P = _____

A = _____   A = _____   A = _____

Check What You Learned

Measurement Concepts

Find the volume of each rectangular solid.

a	b

8. 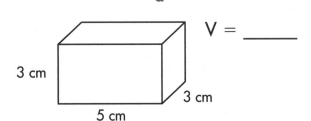 V = _____

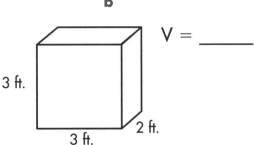 V = _____

SHOW YOUR WORK

Solve each problem.

9. Sandra arrived at school at 7:37 a.m. She left school at 4:32 p.m. How long did Sandra stay at school?

Sandra stayed at school for _____ hours and _____ minutes.

9.

10. Charlie mowed his neighbor's lawn. The lawn is 7 yards long and 5 yards wide. How large an area did Charlie mow?

Charlie mowed _____ square yards.

10.

11. A water tank is 2 meters tall, 5 meters long, and 3 meters wide. The water tank is a rectangular solid. What is its volume?

Its volume is _____ cubic meters.

11.

How much time has elapsed in each problem.

a	b

12. Departure: 7:25 a.m.
    Arrival: 3:42 p.m.
    _____ hours _____ minutes

Departure: 6:15 p.m.
Arrival: 8:28 a.m.
_____ hours _____ minutes

Check What You Know

Geometry

Circle all the regular polygons.

1.

Identify the following quadrilaterals. Write the number that refers to the correct figure.

2. rhombus   _____

3. rectangle   _____

4. trapezoid   _____

5. parallelogram _____

Identify the polygons.

      a   b

6. 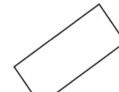 _____  _____

7.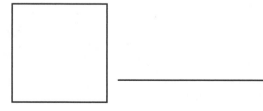

NAME _____

Check What You Know

Geometry

Use a protractor to measure each angle. Then, label each angle *right*, *acute*, or *obtuse*.

a	b

8.

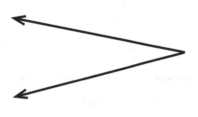

_____   _____

9.

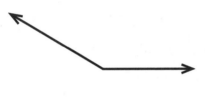

_____   _____

Use the circle to answer the questions.

10. Name the circle. _____

11. Name the origin of the circle. _____

12. Name a radius. _____

13. Name a chord. _____

14. Name a diameter. _____

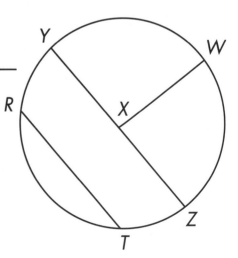

NAME _____

Lesson 9.1 Categories and Subcategories of Figures

Regular polygons are polygons whose sides and angles are equal.

A **rectangle** has 4 right angles.

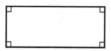

A **quadrilateral** has 4 sides.

A **parallelogram** has 4 sides, and both sets of opposite sides are parallel.

---

1. Circle all the regular polygons.

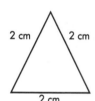 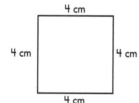 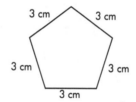 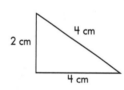 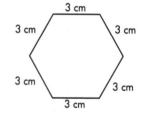

2. Circle all the rectangles.

3. Circle all the quadrilaterals.

  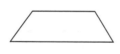 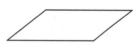

4. Circle all the parallelograms.

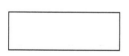    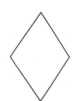

Lesson 9.2 Classifying Quadrilaterals

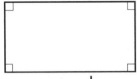   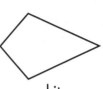

rectangle   square   rhombus   trapezoid   kite

A **rectangle** has four right angles, two pairs of parallel sides, and two pairs of equal sides.

A **square** is a rectangle with four equal sides.

A **rhombus** has two pairs of parallel sides and four equal sides.

A square is a special kind of rectangle and also a special kind of rhombus.

A **trapezoid** has only one pair of parallel sides.

A **kite** has two pairs of equal sides but no parallel sides.

Use the figures below to answer each question. Letters may be used more than once. Some questions will have more than one answer. Some letters may not be used.

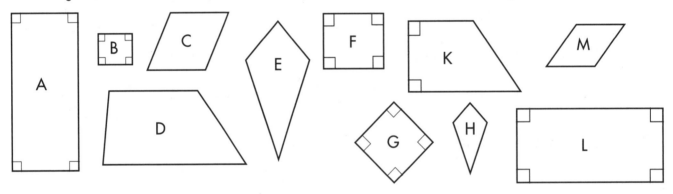

1. Which figure is a rectangle? _____

2. Which figure is a rhombus? _____

3. Which figure is a trapezoid? _____

4. Which figure is a square? _____

5. Which figure is a kite? _____

6. Which figure is both a rhombus and a rectangle? _____

Lesson 9.3 Hierarchy of Figures

polygon	a closed plane figure formed from line segments that meet only at their endpoints
triangle	a three-sided polygon
square	a parallelogram with four equal sides and four right angles
trapezoid	a quadrilateral with exactly one pair of parallel sides
quadrilateral	a four-sided polygon
rhombus	a parallelogram with all four sides equal in length
hexagon	a six-sided polygon
parallelogram	a quadrilateral with both sets of opposites sides parallel
pentagon	a five-sided polygon
rectangle	a quadrilateral with two pairs of equal parallel sides and four right angles

Using the terms above, fill in the blanks to complete the hierarchy diagram.

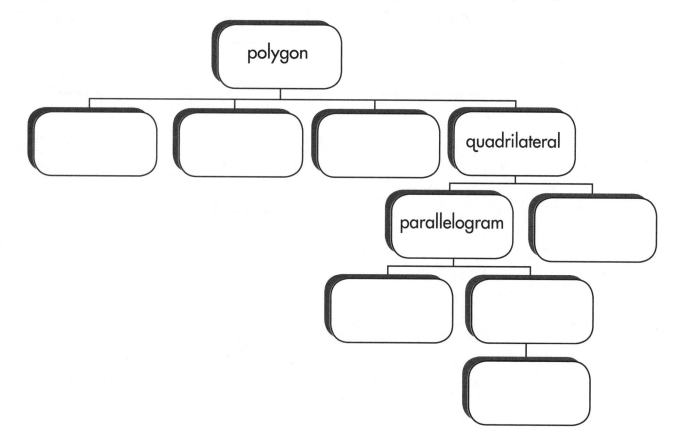

NAME _____

Lesson 9.4 Classifying Angles

A **protractor** is used to measure an angle. The angle is measured in degrees.

A **right angle** measures exactly 90°.

An **acute angle** measures less than 90°.

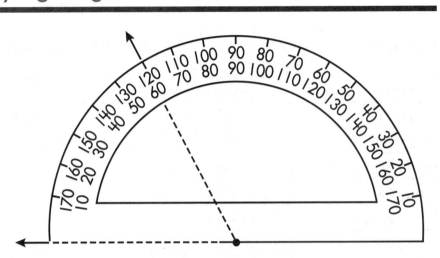

An **obtuse angle** measures greater than 90° but less than 180°.

Identify each angle as *right*, *acute*, or *obtuse*.

	a	**b**

1. Type of Angle _____   Type of Angle _____

2. _____   _____

3. _____   _____

Lesson 9.4 Classifying Angles

Use a protractor to measure each angle. Then, label each angle *right*, *acute*, or *obtuse*.

a	b

1.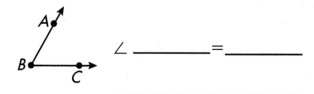

∠ _____ = _____

_____

∠ _____ = _____

_____

2.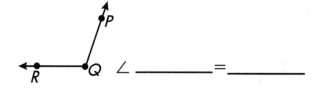

∠ _____ = _____

_____

∠ _____ = _____

_____

3.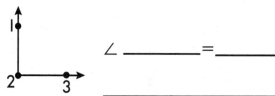

∠ _____ = _____

_____

∠ _____ = _____

_____

Find the measure of each angle of the given triangle. Label each angle as *right*, *acute*, or *obtuse*.

4.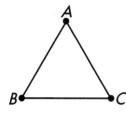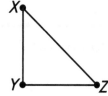

∠ _____ = _____

It is _____.

∠ _____ = _____

It is _____.

∠ _____ = _____

It is _____.

∠ _____ = _____

It is _____.

∠ _____ = _____

It is _____.

∠ _____ = _____

It is _____.

Lesson 9.5 Understanding Circles

The **origin** of a circle is a point inside the circle that is the same distance from any point on the circle. A circle is named by its origin.

A **radius** of a circle is a line segment with one endpoint at the origin and the other endpoint on the circle.

A **chord** is a line segment with both endpoints on the circle.

A **diameter** is a chord that passes through the origin of the circle.

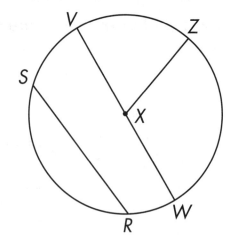

Name a radius, chord, and diameter of circle X.

radius: $\overline{XZ}$, $\overline{XV}$, or $\overline{XW}$ chord: $\overline{VW}$ or $\overline{SR}$ diameter $\overline{VW}$

Identify each line segment as *radius*, *chord*, or *diameter*.

a	b	c	d

1.
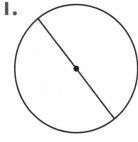 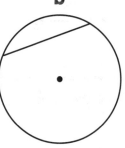 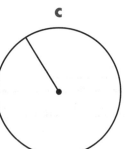 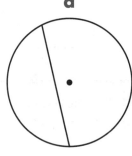

_____   _____   _____   _____

Use the figure at the right to answer the questions.

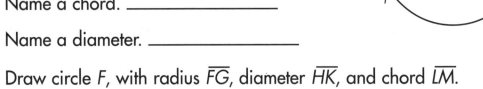

2. Name the circle. _____

3. Name the origin. _____

4. Name a radius. _____

5. Name a chord. _____

6. Name a diameter. _____

7. Draw circle F, with radius $\overline{FG}$, diameter $\overline{HK}$, and chord $\overline{LM}$.

Check What You Learned

Geometry

Circle all the quadrilaterals.

1.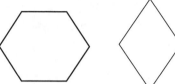

Identify the following polygons. Write the number that refers to the correct figure.

2. parallelogram _____

3. pentagon _____

4. hexagon _____

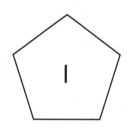 

Fill in the blanks to complete the hierarchy diagram.

5.

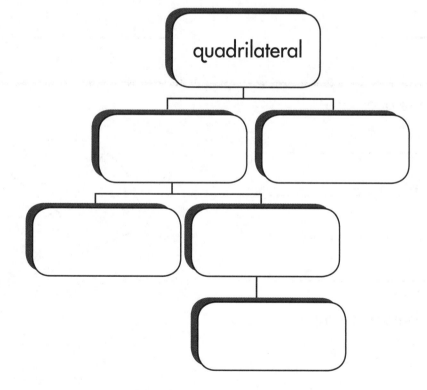

Check What You Learned

Geometry

Use a protractor to measure each angle. Then, label each angle *right*, *acute*, or *obtuse*.

| **a** | **b** |

6.

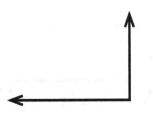

_____   _____

7.

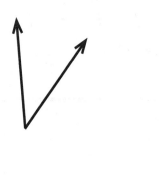

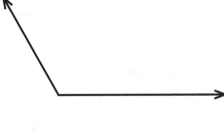

_____   _____

Use the circle to answer the questions.

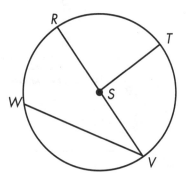

8. Name the circle. _____

9. Name the origin of the circle. _____

10. Name a radius. _____

11. Name a diameter. _____

12. Name a chord that is not a diameter. _____

Check What You Know

Graphing

Identify the ordered pair for each point.

a   **b**

1.

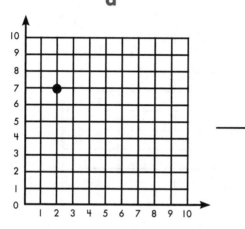   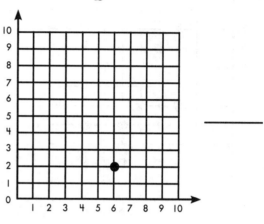

_____   _____

2.

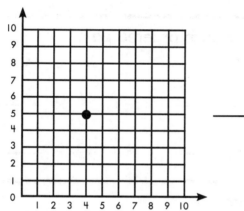   _____

_____

Plot the given points on the grid. Label the points.

3. A (3, 5)   D (4, 6)

C (6, 2)   E (7, 4)

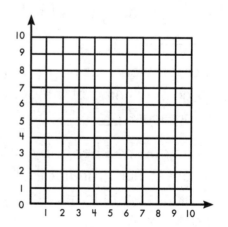

4. F (2, 2)   L (6, 2)

H (6, 5)   I (1, 6)

NAME _____

Check What You Know

Graphing

Use the grids to complete the items below.

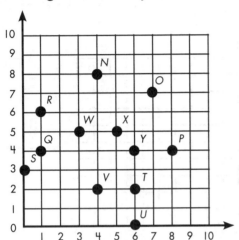

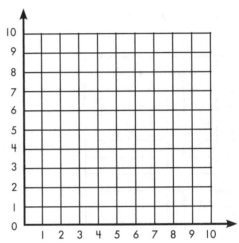

Refer to the grid on the left. Name the point for each ordered pair.

	a	b	c
5.	(0, 3) _____	(3, 5) _____	(6, 0) _____
6.	(4, 8) _____	(8, 4) _____	(5, 5) _____

Use the blank coordinate grid to solve each problem.

7. A line runs from point (1, 7) to (3, 7). How long is the line? _____

8. A square has points (3, 1) and (7, 1). What is the perimeter of the square? _____

9. Carson walks his dog 6 blocks south to the park. Next, they jog 5 blocks east to go swimming at the pond. How many blocks did Carson and his dog travel altogether? _____

10. Ginny pushed her baby sister's stroller 4 blocks west and 3 blocks north to get to her grandmother's house. Then, they walked 5 blocks east and 2 blocks south to the library. How far will they have to walk to get back home? _____

Lesson 10.1 The Coordinate System

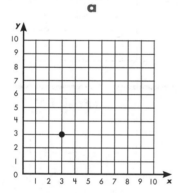

The *x*-axis runs on a horizontal line.

The *y*-axis runs on a vertical line.

Points located on the same grid are called **coordinate points**, or **coordinates**.

A point on a grid is located by using an **ordered pair**. An ordered pair lists the *x*-axis point first and then the *y*-axis point.

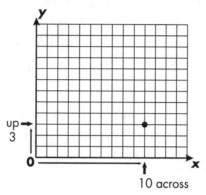

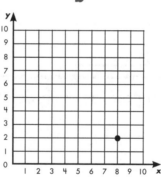

(10, 3)

(*x, y*)

1. Count right ten lines.
2. From that point, go up 3.
3. Draw a point.

Identify the ordered pair from each grid.

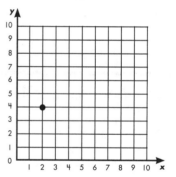

a   b   c

1.

_____   _____   _____

Plot each ordered pair.

2.

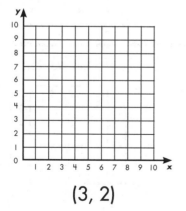

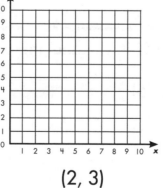

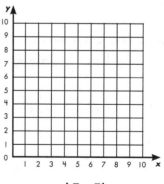

(3, 2)   (2, 3)   (5, 5)

Lesson 10.2 Ordered Pairs

The position of any point of a grid can be described by an **ordered pair** of numbers. The two numbers are named in order: (x, y). Point A on the grid at the right is named by the ordered pair (3, 2). It is located at 3 on the horizontal scale (x) and at 2 on the vertical scale (y). The number on the horizontal scale is always named first in an ordered pair. Point B is named by the ordered pair (7, 3).

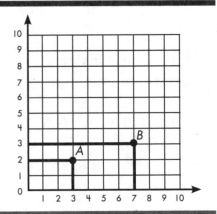

Use Grid 1 to name the point for each ordered pair.

          a   **b**

Grid 1

1. (1, 2) _____   (2, 4) _____

2. (3, 6) _____   (9, 3) _____

3. (9, 0) _____   (5, 5) _____

4. (2, 8) _____   (4, 3) _____

5. (7, 7) _____   (6, 2) _____

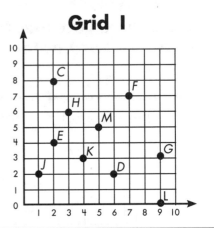

Use Grid 2 to find the ordered pair for each point.

Grid 2

6. B _____   V _____

7. S _____   A _____

8. W _____   N _____

9. T _____   R _____

10. Z _____   P _____

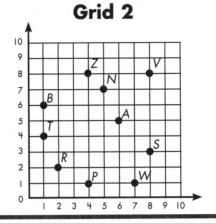

Plot the four points shown on Grid 3. Label the points.

Grid 3

11.   A (2, 4)   D (3, 5)

12.   C (5, 1)   Z (6, 3)

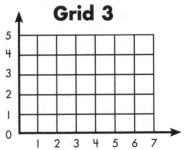

Lesson 10.2 Ordered Pairs

Use the grids to complete the items below.

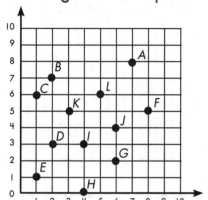
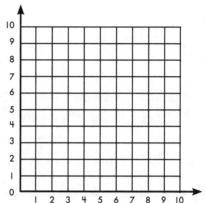

Refer to the grid on the left. Tell what point is located at each ordered pair.

        a   b   c

1.   (3, 5) _____   (4, 0) _____   (8, 5) _____

2.   (2, 7) _____   (5, 6) _____   (1, 1) _____

Refer to the grid on the left. Write the ordered pair for each point.

3.   A (_____)   C (_____)   D (_____)

4.   G (_____)   I (_____)   J (_____)

Plot the points on the grid on the right. Label the points.

5. Create point M at (3, 2).   Create point N at (6, 5).   Create point O at (1, 8).

6. Create point P at (2, 6).   Create point Q at (7, 4).   Create point R at (4, 8).

NAME _____

Lesson 10.3 Problem Solving

You can use coordinate grids to help you solve problems.

A line runs from (3, 2) to (7, 2).
How long is the line?

Count the number of points between the origin
and end of the line to find the length of the line.

The distance between (3, 2) and (7, 2) is 4.

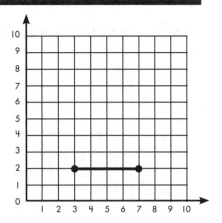

Use the coordinate grid to solve the problems.

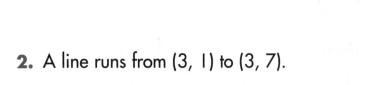

1. A line runs from (2, 8) to (4, 8).

   How long is the line? _____

2. A line runs from (3, 1) to (3, 7).

   How long is the line? _____

3. A rectangle has points at (4, 2), (6, 2),
   (4, 7), and (6, 7).

   What is the perimeter of the rectangle? _____

4. A square has points at (2, 2) and (5, 2).

   What is the perimeter of the square? _____

Lesson 10.3 Problem Solving

You can use coordinate grids to help you solve problems.

Bob rides his bike 4 blocks north, 3 blocks west, and then 4 blocks south. How many blocks will Bob have to ride to get back home?

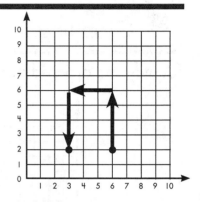

Choose a starting point for Bob (6, 2) and draw lines to show his path and solve the problem.

Bob is 3 blocks from home.

Use the coordinate grid to solve the problems.

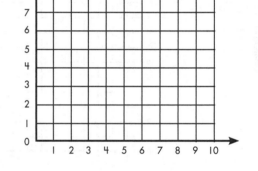

1. Carmen's mom drives her 8 miles north to the store. Then, they go 4 blocks west for lunch and 6 blocks south for dessert. How far will they have to drive to get back home?

   They will have to drive _____ blocks.

2. On her way to school, Tisha walked 2 blocks east to her friend's house. Then, they walked together 5 blocks north to buy snacks. Finally, they walked 3 blocks east and 1 block south to get to school. How far will Tisha have to walk to get home from school if she makes no stops?

   Tisha will have to walk _____ blocks.

3. Kenneth is at point (2, 3). He wants to go to the movies at point (8, 7). He will walk east, then north to get there. Plot Kenneth's starting and ending points. How far will Kenneth walk to get to the movies?

   Kenneth will walk _____ blocks.

4. Shane and Wesley want to meet and play baseball halfway between both of their houses. Shane lives at (4, 1) and Wesley lives at (10, 1). Plot both boys' houses on the grid. At which point should Shane and Wesley meet to play baseball?

   They should meet at point _____.

NAME _____

Check What You Learned

Graphing

Identify the ordered pair for each point.

  a   **b**

1.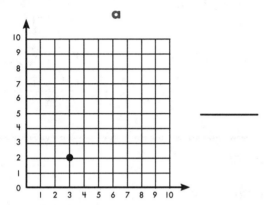

2.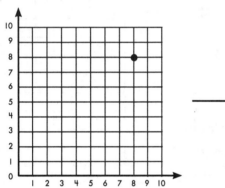

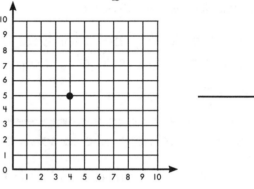

Plot the given points on the grid. Label the points.

3. A (1, 6)   D (4, 10)

     C (5, 4)   E (7, 10)

4. F (1, 1)   L (9,10)

     H (3, 5)   I (0, 7)

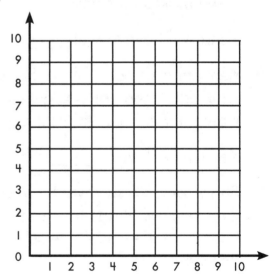

CHAPTER 10 POSTTEST

Spectrum Math
Grade 5

140

Check What You Learned
Chapter 10

Check What You Learned

Graphing

Tell what point on the grid is located at each ordered pair.

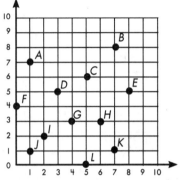

    a   b   c

5. (0, 4) ____   (3, 5) ____   (5, 0) ____

6. (5, 6) ____   (7, 8) ____   (6, 3) ____

Use the coordinate grid to solve each problem.

7. A line runs from point (4, 3) to (10, 3). How long is the line? _____ units

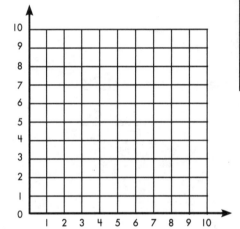

8. A rectangle has points (1, 1), (5, 1), (5, 3), and (1, 3). What is the perimeter of the rectangle? _____

9. Ross's mom tells him to walk to his Aunt Sally's house to bring her some chicken soup. Because Aunt Sally's house is so far away, Ross takes a break halfway at the park. If Ross's house is at (3, 1) and Aunt Sally's house is at (3, 9), at what point is the park? _____ Plot the points to show Ross's house, Aunt Sally's house, and the park.

10. Audrey is meeting her friend at the playground at (1, 7). Audrey lives at (4, 1). Audrey is planning to travel west first and then north. How far does Audrey have to walk to get to the playground?

Audry has to walk _____ units.

Add, subtract, multiply, or divide.

	a	b	c	d
1.	32 × 17	582 × 27	9274 × 216	36944 × 50
2.	24)3218	52)72714	23)1334	44)4092
3.	0.78 + 3.83	$67.52 + 20.18	$16.52 − 6.93	27.63 − 6.39
4.	68.3 × 3.83	22.92 × 2.64	784.58 × 9.16	53.51 × 85.2
5.	0.51)38.76	7.9)64.78	7.13)22.816	9.3)39.99

Spectrum Math
Grade 5
142

Chapters 1–10
Final Test

CHAPTERS 1–10 FINAL TEST

Add, subtract, multiply or divide. Write answers in simplest form.

	a	b	c	d

6.

a. $\dfrac{7}{12} + \dfrac{1}{10}$

b. $\dfrac{2}{5} + \dfrac{4}{5}$

c. $8\dfrac{9}{10} + 9\dfrac{7}{10}$

d. $2\dfrac{1}{2} + 3\dfrac{6}{7}$

7.

a. $\dfrac{5}{8} - \dfrac{1}{8}$

b. $\dfrac{8}{9} - \dfrac{5}{7}$

c. $6 - \dfrac{4}{9}$

d. $7\dfrac{1}{4} - 3\dfrac{1}{3}$

8.

$\dfrac{1}{2} \times \dfrac{4}{7} = \underline{\quad}$
$\dfrac{5}{8} \times \dfrac{3}{5} = \underline{\quad}$
$\dfrac{7}{12} \times \dfrac{3}{8} = \underline{\quad}$
$\dfrac{9}{10} \times \dfrac{10}{11} = \underline{\quad}$

9.

$\dfrac{1}{2} \div 2 = \underline{\quad}$
$5 \div \dfrac{1}{7} = \underline{\quad}$
$\dfrac{1}{9} \div 4 = \underline{\quad}$
$3 \div \dfrac{1}{7} = \underline{\quad}$

10.

$4 \times 1\dfrac{2}{3} = \underline{\quad}$
$2\dfrac{1}{6} \times 7\dfrac{4}{5} = \underline{\quad}$
$4\dfrac{1}{5} \times 3 = \underline{\quad}$
$5\dfrac{1}{7} \times 1\dfrac{5}{9} = \underline{\quad}$

Spectrum Math
Grade 5

Chapters 1–10
Final Test

143

CHAPTERS 1–10 FINAL TEST

Determine the place value of the underlined digit in each number.

	a	b
11.	15.7̲5 _____	1̲2,372 _____
12.	72.05̲ _____	103,7̲28 _____

Round each number to the place of the underlined digit.

13.	103,4̲67 _____	1̲,785,302 _____
14.	23̲,456 _____	103,7̲28 _____

Place the numbers in order from least to greatest.

15. $1.5, 1.7, \dfrac{1}{150}, \dfrac{8}{3}$ _____

16. $0.85, 0.75, \dfrac{5}{6}, \dfrac{2}{3}$ _____

Convert improper fractions into mixed numbers. Convert mixed numbers into improper fractions.

	a	b	c
17.	$\dfrac{29}{12} =$ _____	$\dfrac{23}{5} =$ _____	$\dfrac{10}{4} =$ _____
18.	$4\dfrac{1}{2} =$ _____	$7\dfrac{2}{7} =$ _____	$8\dfrac{1}{8} =$ _____

Complete the table. Then, complete the graph based on the table.

19.

	Add 1	Add 2
30		
31		
32		
33		
34		
35		

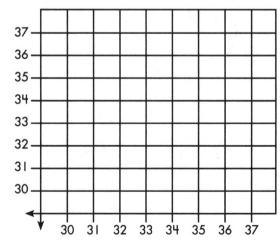

Spectrum Math
Grade 5
144

CHAPTERS 1–10 FINAL TEST

Chapters 1–10
Final Test

Evaluate each expression below.

	a	b
20.	$21 ÷ 3 + (3 × 9) × 9 + 5 =$	$18 ÷ 6 × (4 − 3) + 6 =$
21.	$14 − 8 + 3 + 8 × (24 ÷ 8) =$	$4 × 5 + (14 + 8) − 36 ÷ 9 =$

Find the area and perimeter of each figure.

a	b	c

22.

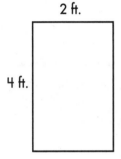

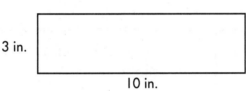

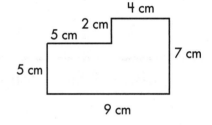

A = _____ sq. ft.   A = _____ sq. in.   A = _____ sq. cm

P = _____ ft.   P = _____ in.   P = _____ cm

Calculate how much time has elapsed in each problem.

a	b

23.   Departure: 5:35 a.m.   Departure: 9:45 p.m.

Arrival: 8:17 p.m.   Arrival: 4:56 a.m.

_____ hours _____ minutes   _____ hours _____ minutes

Spectrum Math
Grade 5

Chapters 1-10
Final Test
145

CHAPTERS 1-10 FINAL TEST

Find the volume of each rectangular prism.

a	b	c

24.

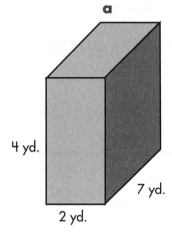
4 yd.
7 yd.
2 yd.

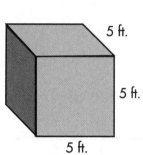
5 ft.
5 ft.
5 ft.

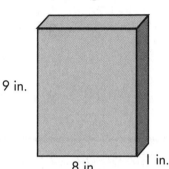
9 in.
8 in.
1 in.

V = _____ cu. yd.   V = _____ cu. ft.   V = _____ cu. in.

---

25. Circle all the rectangles.

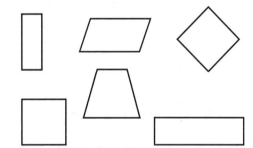

26. Fill in the blanks to complete the hierarchy diagram.

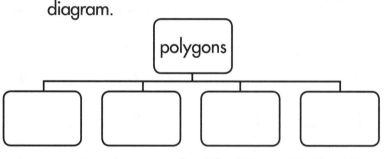

polygons

Refer to the grid to the right. Name the point for each ordered pair.

a	b

27. (6, 4)_____   (1, 8) _____

28. (1, 4)_____   (3, 5) _____

Solve.

29. India's house is at point C. She walks to school, which is at point G. First, she walks east, and then south. How many blocks does India walk to get to school?

India walks _____ blocks to get to school.

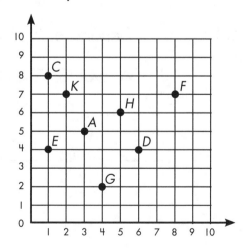

Spectrum Math
Grade 5
146

Chapters 1–10
Final Test

CHAPTERS 1–10 FINAL TEST

Scoring Record for Posttests, Mid-Test, and Final Test

Chapter Posttest	Your Score	Performance			
		Excellent	Very Good	Fair	Needs Improvement
1	_____ of 30	28–30	25–27	19–24	18 or fewer
2	_____ of 30	28–30	25–27	19–24	18 or fewer
3	_____ of 26	25–26	22–24	16–23	15 or fewer
4	_____ of 62	58–62	52–57	39–51	38 or fewer
5	_____ of 21	20–21	18–19	14–17	13 or fewer
6	_____ of 30	28–30	25–27	19–24	18 or fewer
7	_____ of 34	32–34	28–31	22–30	21 or fewer
8	_____ of 24	22–24	20–21	15–19	14 or fewer
9	_____ of 18	17–18	15–16	12–14	11 or fewer
10	_____ of 22	21–22	18–20	16–17	15 or fewer
Mid-Test	_____ of 89	82–89	74–81	56–73	55 or fewer
Final Test	_____ of 94	87–94	78–86	59–77	58 or fewer

Record your test score in the Your Score column. See where you score falls in the Performance columns. Your score is based on the total number of required responses. If your score is fair or needs improvement, review the chapter material.

Grade 5 Answers

Chapter 1

Pretest, page 5

	a	b	c	d
1.	1,715	8,360	26,112	22,080
2.	141,128	83,456	71,154	262,578
3.	78,320	2,168,280	2,241,194	1,627,838
4.	254	60 r3	3	18
5.	27 r23	14 r5	135	37 r6
6.	88 r51	236 r11	34 r63	497 r2

Pretest, page 6

7.	25,145	10.	38
8.	95	11.	33
9.	28,980	12.	147,040

Lesson 1.1, page 7

	a	b	c	d	e	f
1.	1,806	900	1,456	3,276	1,232	273
2.	2,088	3,348	3,072	846	2,607	2,835
3.	1,378	2,886	3,564	30,272	18,832	18,375
4.	48,604	24,738	17,112	51,402	15,836	20,210
5.	29,931	11,205	29,848	29,538	45,818	52,972

Lesson 1.2, page 8

	a	b	c	d	e
1.	13,815	43,428	12,884	69,072	43,518
2.	18,912	35,658	3,708	31,638	13,368
3.	22,578	18,856	104,300	237,318	118,449
4.	339,008	96,025	370,392	253,980	585,488
5.	96,174	402,354	159,360	659,736	239,456

Lesson 1.3, page 9

	a	b	c	d
1.	11 r11	17 r27	8 r76	6 r16
2.	8	5	4 r34	15 r14
3.	9 r18	16 r7	21 r13	11 r22

Lesson 1.4, page 10

	a	b	c	d
1.	152 r35	377	58 r32	54 r21
2.	50 r29	48 r68	109 r20	168
3.	30	202 r1	56 r3	150 r46

Lesson 1.5, page 11

1.	8,000	4.	14,880
2.	2,145	5.	49,029
3.	1,845	6.	141,141

Lesson 1.5, page 12

1.	4	4.	29 (29 r8
2.	3	5.	95 (95 r18)
3.	45 (44 r6)	6.	22 (21 r57)

Posttest, page 13

	a	b	c	d
1.	26,040	30,118	23,856	532,344
2.	69,056	447,714	118,932	247,038
3.	1,181,808	5,165,904	1,031,415	2,108,986
4.	357	2169	8	76 r5
5.	10 r25	4 r33	28	49 r43
6.	177 r39	46 r46	264 r12	33 r75

Posttest, page 14

7.	46	10.	51
8.	44	11.	17,503
9.	837	12.	72,633

Chapter 2

Pretest, page 15

	a	b
1.	300	2,000
2.	4	1
3.	3	1
4.	10,000	1,000,000
5.	8,750	76.43
6.	45,670	34.981
7a.	500,000 + 90,000 + 2,000 + 600 + 80 + 2	
7b.	70 + 8 + 0.3 + 0.06 + 0.004	

Pretest, page 16

	a	b	c
8.	6.203 < 6.214	2.4 = 2.400	48.28 > 46.281
9.	72.355 > 72.335	5.75 < 50.76	9.763 > 9.673
10.	72.1, 72.5, 73.77, 73.943		
11.	42.1, 42.59, 43.2, 43.219		
12.	38.23, 38.4, 38.507, 39.5		
13.	71.3, 71.743, 72.43, 72.5		
14.	3.2	2	5.13
15.	65	9.4	1.23

Lesson 2.1, page 17

	a	b	c	d
1.	5,000,000	50,000	60	5
2.	800,000	7,000	1,000,000	4,000
3.	2,000	40,000	6,000,000	500,000

	a	b
4.	5; hundred thousands	3; millions
5.	6; ten thousands	9; millions
6.	8; hundred thousands	4; millions

Lesson 2.2, page 18

	a	b	c
1.	hundredths	thousands	tenths
2.	tens	thousandths	tenths
3.	ones	hundredths	thousandths

Grade 5 Answers

	a	b	c	d
4.	4	1	5	2
5.	4	3	0	1
6.	3	2	5	1

Lesson 2.3, page 19

	a	b	c
1.	10^5	10^6	10^1
2.	10^7	10^2	10^9
3.	10,000,000	100,000	1,000
4.	100,000,000	1,000,000,000,000	1,000,000

Lesson 2.4, page 20

	a	b	c
1.	214.8	6,070	758
2.	743,400	700	5,020
3.	1.34	0.2765	32.07
4.	0.03457	8.293	0.7269

Lesson 2.5, page 21

1a. 400 + 30
1b. 700 + 20 + 1
2a. 3,000 + 400 + 60 + 5
2b. 40,000 + 3,000 + 600 + 40 + 5
3a. 90,000 + 300 + 20 + 7
3b. 4,000 + 9
4a. 600,000 + 50,000 + 3,000 + 400 + 10
4b. 100,000 + 3,000 + 200 + 50 + 4
5a. 100,000 + 90,000 + 9,000 + 400 + 80 + 2
5b. 30,000 + 2,000 + 400 + 50 + 1
6a. 9,000,000 + 300,000 + 40,000 + 2,000 + 700 + 50 + 1
6b. 2,000,000 + 500,000 + 50 + 5
7a. 500,000 + 90,000 + 8,000 + 700 + 20 + 1
7b. 60,000 + 9,000 + 3

Lesson 2.6, page 22

1a. 200 + 60 + 8 + 0.8 + 0.04 + 0.009
1b. 600 + 50 + 7 + 0.2 + 0.05 + 0.004
2a. 100 + 80 + 2 + 0.1 + 0.09
2b. 9,000 + 900 + 80 + 9 + 0.5 + 0.02
3a. 700 + 50 + 6 + 0.2 + 0.03 + 0.004
3b. 300 + 30 + 2 + 0.1 + 0.01 + 0.005
4a. 400 + 30 + 5 + 0.4 + 0.06 + 0.001
4b. 10 + 4 + 0.5 + 0.01 + 0.004
5a. 2,000 + 900 + 40 + 8 + 0.2 + 0.03
5b. 60 + 9 + 0.2 + 0.04 + 0.001
6a. 200 + 10 + 9 + 0.8 + 0.03 + 0.003
6b. 30,000 + 8,000 + 900 + 60 + 6 + 0.3
7a. 500 + 10 + 9 + 0.5
7b. 900 + 70 + 1 + 0.3 + 0.09 + 0.006

Lesson 2.7, page 23

	a	b	c
1.	5.213 < 5.312	3.1 = 3.10	28.35 > 28.251
2.	6.32 > 6.032	5.17 < 5.172	144.3 > 144
3.	7.325 > 6.425	3.14 > 2.99	48.28 = 48.280
4.	0.213 < 0.223	1.006 < 1.060	0.010 > 0.001
5.	0.674 > 0.644	3.122 < 3.220	43.01 < 43.100
6.	2.897 < 2.90	0.43 = 0.430	0.790 > 0.789
7.	0.571 < 0.58	10.462 < 100.46	9.36 > 9.306
8.	17.110 > 17.101	0.182 < 1.820	98.999 < 99.001
9.	1.090 > 1.009	25.224 < 25.242	63.12 < 63.2
10.	5.703 < 5.730	0.479 < 4.79	81.40 = 81.400

Lesson 2.8, page 24

1. 7.498, 7.52, 7.521, 7.6
2. 0.008, 0.028, 0.080, 0.082
3. 12.191, 12.193, 12.200, 12.201
4. 0.108, 0.113, 0.116, 0.117
5. 22.5, 22.67, 23.703, 23.8
6. 12.13, 12.2, 12.249, 12.5

Lesson 2.9 , page 25

	a	b	c	d
1.	6	6	19	2
2.	45	98	12	73
3.	14	8	1	65
4.	99	270	14	23
5.	96	9	99	52
6.	30	98	33	68

Lesson 2.10 , page 26

	a	b	c	d
1.	7.3	1.2	3.8	6.9
2.	8.0	4.4	5.3	8.2
3.	4.7	5.6	0.1	9.8
4.	5.87	2.21	6.45	1.74
5.	4.40	4.44	9.16	3.48
6.	5.85	4.48	0.99	0.16

Posttest, page 27

	a	b
1.	60	0.007
2.	6	6
3.	9	8
4.	1,000,000,000	100,000
5.	53,240	1.222
6.	4,412	29.3418
7a.	40 + 3 + 0.4 + 0.03 + 0.006	
7b.	3,000 + 600 + 80 + 2 + 0.3	

Grade 5 Answers

Posttest, page 28

	a	b	c
8.	5.113 > 5.112	42.882 < 43.88	4.6 = 4.600
9.	7.295 < 72.95	23.54 > 23.45	9.563 < 9.653
10.	5, 5.6, 6.13, 6.723		
11.	74.2, 74.61, 75, 75.931		
12.	20.35, 20.5, 21.1, 21.967		
13.	46.793, 47.5, 47.7, 47.85		
14.	8	2.2	5.47
15.	3.34	66	9.2

Chapter 3

Pretest, page 29

	a	b	c	d
1.	67.63	754.09	72.11	103.16
2.	39.73	3.57	5.78	51.9
3.	73.71	30.4	119.81	27.1
4.	6.24	7.038	2.5256	8.729
5.	4.2	4	38.6	1,200

Pretest, page 30

6.	2.5		9.	353.8
7.	$41.45		10.	$12.38
8.	$38.97		11.	91.75

Lesson 3.1, page 31

	a	b	c	d
1.	0.9	2.4	2.7	9.8
2.	10.2	8.6	18.6	23.1
3.	1.3	100.4	46.6	45.7
4.	550.5	110.9	562	113.3
5.	0.4	1.7	42.2	72.2
6.	151.3	466.5	34.4	42.8

Lesson 3.2, page 32

	a	b	c	d
1.	11.7	1.61	4.23	9.81
2.	2.31	40.21	44.33	10.52
3.	10.45	70.79	134.99	33.5
4.	8.1	77.16	46.33	101.1
5.	15.22	590.13	204.11	28.2
6.	0.76	12.59	94.2	8.13
7.	6.89	0.91	1.55	6.92

Lesson 3.3, page 33

	a	b	c	d	e
1.	71.1	30.2	0.1	0.1	2.7
2.	235.1	85.9	1.2	53.3	93.1
3.	21.9	32.1	2.8	81	0.02
4.	7.3	28.6	1.2	0.9	1.8
5.	2.8	18.2	2.6	2.6	5.3
6.	2.2	2.2	33.6	56.8	40.8

Lesson 3.4, page 34

	a	b	c	d	e
1.	0.5	0.8	1.9	0.69	1.5
2.	7.04	0.16	0.33	1.3	2.8
3.	16.3	0.37	0.33	2.57	7.11
4.	4.22	14.4	24.23	5.9	7.76
5.	16.8	9.14	26.16	41.7	95.3
6.	1.86	1.46	2.69	1.3	4.9
7.	69.2	36.46	5.54	3.7	6.17

Lesson 3.5, page 35

	a	b	c	d	e
1.	2.35	1.58	15.96	52.86	9.24
2.	0.47	1.26	2.36	3.21	10.15
3.	17.37	31.55	8.94	7.73	12.11
4.	6.09	8.84	11.04	12.06	29.61
5.	13.22	1.02	5.00	8.91	11.37
6.	57.96	0.64	94.86	2.79	8.03
7.	12.37	15.27	18.05	6.01	0.07

Lesson 3.6, page 36

1.	$7.60	4.	$0.90
2.	$580.15	5.	$132.15
3.	$1.20	6.	$4.75

Lesson 3.7, page 37

1. 0.21

2. 0.14

3. 0.32

Lesson 3.8, page 38

	a	b	c
1.	3	2	2
2.	1	4	3

	a	b	c	d
3.	4,901.<u>5488</u>	1,232.84	1,263.<u>9382</u>	1,875.<u>104</u>
4.	3,731.<u>9211</u>	4,689.<u>75</u>	7,390.<u>66</u>	255.<u>36</u>

Grade 5 Answers

Lesson 3.9, page 39

	a	b	c	d	e
1.	3.6	2.44	6.96	3.63	65.4
2.	5.55	17.472	2.8721	2.628	4.475
3.	5.566	1.46	30.102	5.13	4.401
4.	18.21	2.328	2.121	3.48	44.52
5.	6.8	7.92	128.184	.0648	11.892

Lesson 3.10, page 40

1. 3
2. 4
3. 2
4. 2

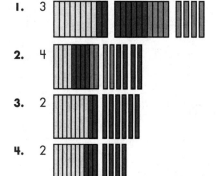

Lesson 3.11, page 41

	a	b	c
1.	100; 17	100; 15	10; 1.6
2.	100; 9	100; 13	10; .9
3.	100; 8.8	10; 1.8	100; 13
4.	10; 1.9	10; 16	10; 1.8

Lesson 3.12, page 42

	a	b	c	d
1.	1,520	12	4.4	3.74
2.	3.9	63	36.5	6.6
3.	31.5	328	5.6	4.225
4.	1.4	2.125	18	1.6

Lesson 3.13, page 43

1. $14.95   5. $64.93
2. 14.5   6. 0.806
3. 17.5   7. 0.88
4. 127.75

Posttest, page 44

	a	b	c	d
1.	1.13	79.41	11.84	57.81
2.	26.98	5.09	2.42	26.29
3.	1.85	27.46	38.8	137.41
4.	2.48	8.6315	16.2159	4.433
5.	260	475	18.9	2.2

Posttest, page 45

6. $36.65   9. $3.53
7. 9   10. 8.8
8. 0.24   11. 29.16

Chapter 4

Pretest, page 46

	a	b	c	d	e
1.	$5\frac{2}{5}$	$4\frac{3}{8}$	$2\frac{1}{7}$	$6\frac{1}{4}$	$5\frac{2}{3}$
2.	$\frac{53}{16}$	$\frac{18}{5}$	$\frac{17}{7}$	$\frac{19}{16}$	$\frac{13}{3}$
3.	2	25	18	8	8
4.	5	6	2	1	8
5.	24	60	20	24	12
6.	30	60	60	120	10

Pretest, page 47

	a	b	c	d
7.	$\frac{2}{3}$	$\frac{1}{3}$	$\frac{5}{8}$	$\frac{3}{7}$
8.	$\frac{5}{6}$	$\frac{8}{9}$	$\frac{6}{7}$	$\frac{1}{2}$
9.	8	2	10	25
10.	8	42	66	28
11.	$\frac{8}{10} > \frac{1}{12}$	$\frac{2}{3} > \frac{1}{2}$	$\frac{6}{9} > \frac{2}{5}$	$\frac{4}{6} > \frac{5}{9}$
12.	$\frac{3}{6} < \frac{7}{9}$	$\frac{2}{5} > \frac{1}{4}$	$\frac{2}{7} < \frac{2}{3}$	$\frac{6}{7} > \frac{1}{5}$
13.	0.4	0.5	0.25	0.875
14.	$\frac{1}{2}$	$\frac{3}{5}$	$\frac{3}{4}$	$\frac{5}{8}$

Lesson 4.1, page 48

1. $4, \frac{3}{4}$ 3. $21 \div 3, \frac{21}{3}, 7$
2. $45 \div 5, \frac{45}{5}, 9$ 4. $25, \frac{2}{5}$

Lesson 4.2, page 49

	a	b	c
1.	$1\frac{2}{3}$	$1\frac{1}{6}$	$1\frac{4}{5}$
2.	$1\frac{1}{2}$	$1\frac{1}{3}$	$1\frac{3}{5}$
3.	$1\frac{2}{5}$	$1\frac{2}{7}$	$1\frac{1}{4}$
4.	$5\frac{1}{3}$	$12\frac{3}{4}$	$5\frac{4}{9}$
5.	$13\frac{1}{5}$	$27\frac{2}{3}$	$5\frac{3}{5}$
6.	$9\frac{2}{3}$	4	$10\frac{2}{3}$

Lesson 4.3, page 50

	a	b	c	d
1.	$\frac{21}{8}$	$\frac{13}{4}$	$\frac{17}{7}$	$\frac{5}{1}$
2.	$\frac{15}{4}$	$\frac{29}{12}$	$\frac{25}{6}$	$\frac{17}{3}$
3.	$\frac{39}{16}$	$\frac{7}{2}$	$\frac{23}{16}$	$\frac{21}{8}$
4.	$\frac{10}{3}$	$\frac{22}{5}$	$\frac{25}{8}$	$\frac{22}{3}$
5.	$\frac{26}{3}$	$\frac{7}{5}$	$\frac{17}{7}$	$\frac{35}{9}$
6.	$\frac{22}{5}$	$\frac{23}{6}$	$\frac{22}{9}$	$\frac{53}{12}$

Lesson 4.4, page 51

	a	b
1.	14	9
2.	12	5
3.	18	7
4.	2	11
5.	14	20
6.	20	30
7.	12	18
8.	10	55

Grade 5 Answers

Lesson 4.5, page 52

	a	b	c
1.	$\frac{3}{12}, \frac{8}{12}$	$\frac{15}{40}, \frac{28}{40}$	$\frac{12}{21}, \frac{14}{21}$
2.	$\frac{9}{24}, \frac{4}{24}$	$\frac{4}{6}, \frac{3}{6}$	$\frac{9}{24}, \frac{20}{24}$
3.	$\frac{6}{15}, \frac{5}{15}$	$\frac{5}{16}, \frac{6}{16}$	$\frac{3}{6}, \frac{2}{6}$
4.	$\frac{10}{16}, \frac{3}{16}$	$\frac{8}{20}, \frac{15}{20}$	$\frac{25}{60}, \frac{48}{60}$
5.	$\frac{10}{18}, \frac{9}{18}$	$\frac{21}{24}, \frac{14}{24}$	$\frac{1}{9}, \frac{6}{9}$

Lesson 4.6, page 53

	a	b	c
1.	2	9	6
2.	12	6	35
3.	35	15	6
4.	27	24	25
5.	18	14	48

Lesson 4.7, page 54

	a	b	c
1.	$\frac{1}{2}$	$\frac{1}{2}$	$\frac{1}{2}$
2.	$\frac{1}{4}$	$\frac{1}{3}$	$\frac{1}{5}$
3.	$\frac{1}{5}$	$\frac{4}{5}$	$\frac{1}{4}$
4.	$\frac{1}{2}$	$\frac{13}{14}$	$\frac{1}{4}$
5.	$\frac{5}{7}$	$\frac{17}{25}$	$\frac{7}{9}$
6.	$\frac{11}{32}$	$\frac{7}{9}$	$\frac{1}{4}$

Lesson 4.8, page 55

	a	b	c	d
1.	$3\frac{3}{4}$	$2\frac{4}{5}$	$1\frac{3}{4}$	$4\frac{2}{3}$
2.	$3\frac{3}{5}$	$6\frac{3}{4}$	$3\frac{1}{3}$	$4\frac{1}{2}$
3.	$4\frac{1}{2}$	$5\frac{2}{5}$	$8\frac{3}{5}$	$7\frac{1}{4}$
4.	$4\frac{1}{2}$	$4\frac{1}{2}$	$7\frac{2}{3}$	$5\frac{1}{3}$
5.	$5\frac{1}{3}$	$5\frac{1}{5}$	$5\frac{1}{7}$	$4\frac{2}{9}$

Lesson 4.9, page 56

	a	b	c	d
1.	$\frac{19}{9} > \frac{1}{10}$	$1\frac{1}{12} < 10\frac{1}{3}$	$2\frac{1}{9} < 10\frac{1}{2}$	$\frac{1}{9} < \frac{6}{7}$
2.	$\frac{4}{6} > \frac{5}{9}$	$\frac{4}{7} < \frac{21}{11}$	$\frac{29}{9} > 2\frac{1}{6}$	$\frac{26}{11} > \frac{22}{11}$
3.	$\frac{20}{8} > \frac{12}{8}$	$\frac{4}{9} < 7\frac{1}{4}$	$2\frac{11}{12} > 1\frac{1}{5}$	$\frac{4}{2} < \frac{29}{9}$
4.	$\frac{2}{2} > \frac{1}{3}$	$\frac{1}{3} < 2\frac{11}{12}$	$5\frac{1}{2} > \frac{11}{12}$	$\frac{13}{3} > \frac{1}{5}$
5.	$\frac{2}{5} < 2\frac{3}{8}$	$\frac{20}{11} < \frac{25}{22}$	$\frac{1}{7} < 7\frac{1}{3}$	$\frac{1}{9} < \frac{19}{6}$
6.	$3\frac{2}{10} < \frac{26}{8}$	$\frac{2}{3} > \frac{1}{2}$	$\frac{5}{9} > \frac{1}{9}$	$\frac{19}{9} < \frac{27}{4}$
7.	$\frac{1}{7}, \frac{6}{7}, 1\frac{1}{7}, 1\frac{2}{3}, 1\frac{8}{9}$			
8.	$\frac{2}{7}, \frac{4}{7}, \frac{7}{8}, 1\frac{1}{4}, 1\frac{1}{2}$			
9.	$\frac{1}{6}, \frac{5}{6}, 1\frac{1}{3}, 1\frac{4}{7}, 1\frac{7}{8}$			

Lesson 4.10, page 57

	a	b	c
1.	0.4	0.40	0.400
2.	3.5	0.12	0.680
3.	2.6	0.45	0.116
4.	2.2	0.34	1.270
5.	0.8	0.75	0.075
6.	7.5	2.30	0.056

Lesson 4.11, page 58

	a	b	c	d
1.	$\frac{2}{5}$	$\frac{3}{4}$	$3\frac{1}{10}$	$\frac{3}{5}$
2.	$\frac{1}{4}$	$1\frac{3}{10}$	$4\frac{3}{20}$	$2\frac{1}{5}$
3.	$3\frac{1}{8}$	$\frac{4}{25}$	$8\frac{2}{5}$	$2\frac{1}{2}$
4.	$\frac{1}{1000}$	$\frac{1}{25}$	$1\frac{3}{5}$	$1\frac{1}{100}$
5.	$\frac{16}{25}$	$\frac{7}{10}$	$4\frac{3}{5}$	$\frac{22}{25}$
6.	$2\frac{21}{50}$	$\frac{14}{25}$	$\frac{3}{20}$	$\frac{1}{500}$
7.	$2\frac{3}{10}$	$3\frac{9}{10}$	$1\frac{19}{20}$	$\frac{221}{500}$
8.	$1\frac{43}{50}$	$3\frac{31}{100}$	$\frac{24}{25}$	$\frac{3}{25}$
9.	$4\frac{19}{25}$	$3\frac{89}{100}$	$4\frac{2}{25}$	$\frac{11}{20}$

Posttest, page 59

	a	b	c	d	e
1.	$5\frac{1}{2}$	$1\frac{1}{8}$	$2\frac{5}{6}$	$2\frac{5}{9}$	$2\frac{1}{6}$
2.	$2\frac{2}{7}$	$8\frac{1}{3}$	$1\frac{3}{7}$	$4\frac{2}{7}$	$2\frac{3}{4}$
3.	$\frac{30}{8}$	$\frac{116}{12}$	$\frac{63}{14}$	$\frac{51}{8}$	$\frac{25}{8}$
4.	$\frac{11}{4}$	$\frac{62}{9}$	$\frac{107}{12}$	$\frac{40}{9}$	$\frac{37}{7}$
5.	8	7	9	1	3
6.	12	12	60	30	30

Posttest, page 60

	a	b	c	d
7.	$\frac{2}{5}$	$\frac{3}{5}$	$\frac{5}{8}$	$\frac{4}{5}$
8.	$\frac{7}{8}$	$\frac{2}{7}$	$\frac{5}{8}$	$\frac{8}{9}$
9.	35	72	32	21
10.	49	15	18	36
11.	$\frac{8}{6} > \frac{6}{4}$	$\frac{10}{8} > \frac{6}{5}$	$\frac{7}{9} > \frac{6}{8}$	$\frac{12}{10} = \frac{6}{5}$
12.	$\frac{4}{6} < \frac{10}{5}$	$\frac{4}{6} > \frac{5}{6}$	$\frac{8}{5} > \frac{10}{8}$	$\frac{4}{9} < \frac{4}{5}$
13.	0.4	0.6	0.5	0.3
14.	$7\frac{13}{50}$	$10\frac{2}{5}$	$\frac{7}{10}$	$6\frac{1}{4}$

Chapter 5

Pretest, page 61

	a	b	c	d
1.	$\frac{7}{8}$	$\frac{6}{7}$	$\frac{1}{2}$	$\frac{7}{9}$
2.	$1\frac{1}{20}$	1	$11\frac{8}{9}$	$7\frac{37}{40}$
3.	$\frac{3}{4}$	$\frac{1}{9}$	$\frac{1}{2}$	$\frac{1}{2}$
4.	$\frac{1}{8}$	$\frac{2}{35}$	$\frac{22}{63}$	$4\frac{1}{12}$

Pretest, page 62

5.	$6\frac{3}{8}$
6.	$4\frac{1}{3}$
7.	$\frac{25}{63}$
8.	$1\frac{13}{20}$
9.	$\frac{5}{9}$

Grade 5 Answers

Lesson 5.1, page 63

	a	b	c	d
1.	$\frac{3}{5}$	$\frac{2}{7}$	$\frac{1}{2}$	$\frac{3}{4}$
2.	$\frac{1}{2}$	$\frac{4}{5}$	$\frac{1}{2}$	$\frac{2}{5}$
3.	$\frac{2}{3}$	$\frac{7}{9}$	$\frac{6}{7}$	$\frac{2}{3}$
4.	$\frac{2}{5}$	$\frac{1}{9}$	$\frac{5}{7}$	$\frac{2}{3}$

Lesson 5.2, page 64

	a	b	c	d	e
1.	$\frac{17}{20}$	$\frac{20}{21}$	$\frac{12}{35}$	$\frac{13}{24}$	$\frac{5}{6}$
2.	$\frac{61}{72}$	$1\frac{4}{21}$	$1\frac{4}{35}$	$1\frac{4}{30}$	$\frac{31}{56}$
3.	$\frac{13}{15}$	$1\frac{8}{63}$	$1\frac{1}{20}$	$1\frac{11}{40}$	$1\frac{47}{63}$

Lesson 5.2, page 65

	a	b	c	d	e
1.	$1\frac{1}{4}$	$1\frac{1}{10}$	$1\frac{7}{12}$	$1\frac{1}{6}$	$\frac{3}{4}$
2.	$\frac{5}{8}$	$1\frac{2}{9}$	$1\frac{7}{24}$	$1\frac{1}{5}$	$1\frac{7}{12}$
3.	1	$1\frac{1}{24}$	$\frac{21}{40}$	$1\frac{5}{36}$	$1\frac{13}{18}$
4.	$\frac{7}{10}$	$1\frac{1}{2}$	$1\frac{1}{12}$	$\frac{11}{24}$	$\frac{24}{35}$

Lesson 5.3, page 66

	a	b	c	d	e
1.	$\frac{1}{4}$	$\frac{1}{2}$	$\frac{1}{2}$	$\frac{25}{56}$	$\frac{2}{9}$
2.	$\frac{13}{45}$	$\frac{11}{35}$	$\frac{7}{24}$	$\frac{1}{2}$	$\frac{19}{36}$
3.	$\frac{1}{5}$	$\frac{23}{26}$	$\frac{11}{24}$	$\frac{9}{20}$	$\frac{13}{35}$

Lesson 5.3, page 67

	a	b	c	d
1.	$\frac{5}{18}$	$\frac{3}{8}$	$\frac{1}{18}$	$\frac{1}{16}$
2.	$\frac{13}{30}$	$\frac{11}{30}$	$\frac{9}{35}$	$\frac{1}{4}$
3.	$\frac{37}{72}$	$\frac{7}{30}$	$\frac{1}{126}$	$\frac{131}{1260}$
4.	$\frac{8}{45}$	$\frac{1}{120}$	$\frac{1}{104}$	$\frac{29}{56}$

Lesson 5.4, page 68

	a	b	c	d
1.	$5\frac{9}{10}$	$7\frac{13}{15}$	$8\frac{1}{28}$	$7\frac{9}{20}$
2.	$9\frac{31}{42}$	$9\frac{13}{30}$	$10\frac{17}{24}$	$13\frac{13}{18}$
3.	$16\frac{11}{24}$	$14\frac{17}{21}$	$10\frac{61}{63}$	$9\frac{2}{15}$

Lesson 5.4, page 69

	a	b	c	d
1.	$5\frac{7}{10}$	$8\frac{1}{8}$	$7\frac{1}{6}$	$6\frac{1}{3}$
2.	$3\frac{11}{12}$	$6\frac{1}{8}$	$4\frac{1}{2}$	$4\frac{7}{8}$
3.	$14\frac{11}{30}$	$14\frac{31}{45}$	$12\frac{1}{24}$	$19\frac{43}{70}$
4.	$4\frac{7}{12}$	$8\frac{1}{8}$	$4\frac{5}{12}$	$7\frac{1}{8}$
5.	$7\frac{1}{3}$	4	$8\frac{3}{8}$	$6\frac{23}{30}$

Lesson 5.5, page 70

	a	b	c	d	e
1.	$2\frac{1}{2}$	$5\frac{1}{8}$	$2\frac{1}{2}$	$4\frac{3}{8}$	$1\frac{1}{9}$
2.	$2\frac{11}{56}$	$4\frac{1}{3}$	$5\frac{19}{40}$	$6\frac{2}{9}$	$3\frac{9}{70}$
3.	$5\frac{11}{12}$	$3\frac{7}{40}$	$3\frac{5}{12}$	$3\frac{9}{35}$	$2\frac{3}{4}$

Lesson 5.5, page 71

	a	b	c	d
1.	$3\frac{5}{8}$	$4\frac{1}{2}$	$4\frac{3}{8}$	$4\frac{3}{10}$
2.	$1\frac{1}{8}$	$4\frac{1}{2}$	$2\frac{1}{12}$	$5\frac{3}{10}$
3.	$2\frac{1}{2}$	$\frac{1}{2}$	$4\frac{3}{5}$	$\frac{2}{3}$
4.	$1\frac{7}{8}$	$2\frac{5}{6}$	2	$2\frac{1}{6}$
5.	$1\frac{3}{22}$	$3\frac{13}{40}$	$1\frac{47}{72}$	$1\frac{1}{6}$

Lesson 5.6, page 72

1. $6\frac{2}{63}$	3. $\frac{7}{12}$	5. $6\frac{11}{21}$
2. $13\frac{4}{15}$	4. $6\frac{9}{40}$	6. $10\frac{7}{12}$

Lesson 5.6, page 73

1. $\frac{3}{14}$	3. $1\frac{1}{3}$	5. $\frac{19}{24}$
2. $\frac{17}{20}$	4. $\frac{3}{8}$	6. $1\frac{7}{15}$

Posttest, page 74

	a	b	c	d
1.	$\frac{5}{6}$	$\frac{5}{7}$	$\frac{8}{9}$	$1\frac{1}{8}$
2.	$1\frac{11}{60}$	$1\frac{3}{10}$	$13\frac{1}{15}$	$17\frac{4}{5}$
3.	$\frac{1}{3}$	$\frac{1}{7}$	$\frac{3}{8}$	$\frac{1}{4}$
4.	$3\frac{1}{6}$	$2\frac{1}{3}$	$1\frac{1}{28}$	$7\frac{14}{45}$

Posttest, page 75

5. $1\frac{1}{6}$	7. $4\frac{9}{20}$	9. $\frac{3}{4}$
6. $5\frac{1}{4}$	8. $2\frac{1}{6}$	

Mid-Test

Mid-Test, page 76

	a	b	c	d
1.	15,400	2,808	58,378	243,852
2.	9	20 r4	118 r11	169
3.	7.54	34.95	144.87	204.74
4.	26.2	6.33	71.71	8.91
5.	2,168.2	1.68	9.1	289.556

Mid-Test, page 77

	a	b	c	d
6.	39.2	2,368	63.18	550.68
7.	4	1,200	0.8	0.7
8.	5.2	8	7	4
9a.	700 + 30 + 2			
9b.	30,000 + 2,000+ 100 + 30 + 2			
9c.	4,000 + 700 + 90			
10a.	10 + 0.03			
10b.	20,000 + 3,000 + 100 + 40 + 7 + 0.3 + 0.02			
10c.	300 + 0.1			

	a	b	c
11.	30	90,000	5,000
12.	3,000,000	0.04	0.2

Grade 5 Answers

Mid-Test, page 78

	a	b	c	d
13.	1	$\frac{31}{35}$	$1\frac{5}{24}$	$5\frac{2}{3}$
14.	$\frac{1}{2}$	0	$\frac{6}{55}$	$6\frac{1}{4}$
15.	$7\frac{5}{12}$	$17\frac{1}{21}$	$12\frac{3}{8}$	$3\frac{23}{24}$
16.	$4\frac{1}{6}$	$4\frac{1}{36}$	$2\frac{1}{2}$	$4\frac{5}{6}$

	a	b	c
17.	$\frac{9}{10}$	$\frac{4}{5}$	$2\frac{1}{6}$
18.	$3\frac{2}{3}$	$8\frac{1}{2}$	$7\frac{2}{3}$

Mid-Test, page 79

	a	b	c
19.	$2\frac{1}{4}$	$5\frac{2}{3}$	$11\frac{1}{3}$
20.	$4\frac{5}{12}$	$10\frac{1}{4}$	$9\frac{3}{7}$
21.	$\frac{13}{3}$	$\frac{68}{9}$	$\frac{17}{10}$
22.	$\frac{15}{4}$	$\frac{71}{12}$	$\frac{74}{9}$

	a	b	c	d
23.	$\frac{7}{8} < \frac{9}{10}$	$\frac{1}{4} < \frac{4}{10}$	$\frac{2}{3} < \frac{9}{10}$	$\frac{8}{10} > \frac{2}{3}$

24a. $80.59 < 80.67$ 25. $0.1, \frac{1}{4}, \frac{1}{3}, 3.1$

24b. $46.94 > 46.37$ 26. $\frac{1}{9}, 0.5, \frac{5}{8}, 0.7$

24c. $54.72 > 54.27$ 27. $\frac{1}{150}, \frac{3}{2}, 1.7, \frac{8}{3}$

24d. $86.4 = 86.40$

Chapter 6

Pretest, page 80

	a	b	c
1.	$\frac{1}{6}$	$\frac{3}{14}$	$\frac{1}{5}$
2.	$\frac{1}{4}$	$\frac{2}{9}$	$1\frac{3}{7}$
3.	$1\frac{1}{2}$	$3\frac{1}{9}$	$1\frac{1}{2}$
4.	$5\frac{1}{2}$	$4\frac{1}{8}$	3
5.	60	$\frac{1}{112}$	4
6.	$\frac{1}{18}$	$\frac{1}{30}$	28
7.	$\frac{1}{20}$	88	$\frac{1}{18}$
8.	15	$\frac{1}{24}$	72

Pretest, page 81

9. $\frac{8}{15}$ 11. $\frac{3}{4}$ 13. $12\frac{4}{9}$

10. $\frac{1}{2}$ 12. 16   14. $50\frac{2}{5}$

Lesson 6.1, page 82

	a	b	c
1.	$\frac{3}{8}$	$3\frac{1}{3}$	$1\frac{7}{9}$

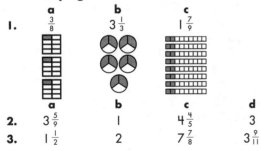

	a	b	c	d
2.	$3\frac{5}{9}$	1	$4\frac{4}{5}$	3
3.	$1\frac{1}{2}$	2	$7\frac{7}{8}$	$3\frac{9}{11}$

Lesson 6.2, page 83

	a	b	c
1.	$\frac{2}{27}$	$\frac{1}{20}$	$\frac{9}{28}$
2.	$\frac{5}{16}$	$\frac{5}{21}$	$\frac{1}{11}$
3.	$\frac{2}{5}$	$\frac{1}{7}$	$\frac{4}{27}$
4.	$\frac{14}{25}$	$\frac{1}{4}$	$\frac{5}{22}$
5.	$\frac{5}{9}$	$\frac{27}{40}$	$\frac{49}{132}$

Lesson 6.3, page 84

	a	b	c	d
1.	$5\frac{1}{6}$	$6\frac{5}{12}$	$15\frac{1}{6}$	$4\frac{20}{21}$
2.	$8\frac{3}{40}$	$14\frac{32}{35}$	$5\frac{4}{9}$	$14\frac{2}{27}$
3.	$12\frac{3}{5}$	$8\frac{13}{15}$	$21\frac{5}{7}$	$14\frac{34}{49}$
4.	$20\frac{5}{12}$	$5\frac{5}{64}$	9	$12\frac{4}{15}$
5.	$4\frac{35}{72}$	$16\frac{1}{4}$	$6\frac{29}{32}$	39

Lesson 6.4, page 85

	a	b
1.	$\frac{1}{28}$	$\frac{1}{9}$
2.	$\frac{1}{45}$	$\frac{1}{12}$
3.	$\frac{1}{14}$	$\frac{1}{12}$

Lesson 6.5, page 86

	a	b	c	d
1.	$\frac{1}{9}$	$\frac{1}{40}$	$\frac{1}{30}$	$\frac{1}{24}$
2.	$\frac{1}{36}$	$\frac{1}{14}$	$\frac{1}{90}$	$\frac{1}{36}$
3.	$\frac{1}{48}$	$\frac{1}{40}$	$\frac{1}{48}$	$\frac{1}{40}$
4.	$\frac{1}{60}$	$\frac{1}{49}$	$\frac{1}{48}$	$\frac{1}{60}$

Lesson 6.6, page 87

	a	b	c	d
1.	15	48	10	56
2.	36	60	75	32
3.	20	45	25	110
4.	48	54	21	60

Lesson 6.6, page 88

	a	b	c	d
1.	12	60	114	60
2.	68	144	54	14
3.	10	70	40	64
4.	14	80	65	36
5.	35	27	120	42
6.	22	57	72	90

Lesson 6.7, page 89

1. $\frac{8}{15}$ 3. $1\frac{1}{3}$ 5. $\frac{3}{7}$

2. $\frac{1}{12}$ 4. $2\frac{1}{12}$ 6. 14

Lesson 6.7, page 90

1. 32   4. $\frac{1}{24}$

2. $\frac{1}{28}$ 5. 21

3. 72   6. 8

Grade 5 Answers

Posttest, page 91

	a	b	c
1.	$\frac{2}{9}$	$\frac{1}{2}$	$\frac{5}{14}$
2.	$\frac{11}{18}$	$\frac{12}{35}$	$\frac{9}{32}$
3.	$1\frac{7}{8}$	$\frac{2}{3}$	3
4.	$5\frac{3}{4}$	$14\frac{1}{4}$	$26\frac{2}{5}$
5.	48	$\frac{1}{36}$	20
6.	$\frac{1}{30}$	$\frac{1}{20}$	16
7.	$\frac{1}{30}$	15	$\frac{1}{24}$
8.	$\frac{1}{21}$	50	$\frac{1}{84}$

Posttest, page 92

9.	$\frac{1}{35}$	11. $1\frac{5}{18}$	13. $9\frac{4}{5}$
10.	$\frac{1}{4}$	12. $\frac{1}{56}$	14. $\frac{1}{42}$

Chapter 7

Pretest, page 93

1.
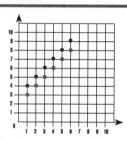

	Add 2	Add 3
1	3	4
2	4	5
3	5	6
4	6	7
5	7	8
6	8	9

	a	b
2.	30	20
3.	3	18
4.	5	16
5.	95	32
6.	108	24
7.	61	6

Posttest, page 94

8. $6 + 2 \times 3 =$
9. $8 \div (3 + 1) =$
10. $4 + 25 \div 5 =$
11. $21 - (3 \times 4) =$
12. $\$10.00 - (\$3.95 + \$1.50 + \$1.25 + \$0.47) = \$2.83$
13. $3 \times (3 + 5 + 8) = 48$

Lesson 7.1, page 95

1.
	Add 2	Add 4
21	23	25
22	24	26
23	25	27
24	26	28
25	27	29
26	28	30

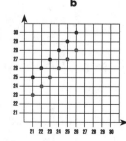

(page 2 table)

2.
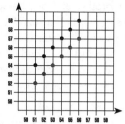

	Add 1	Add 3
51	52	54
52	53	55
53	54	56
54	55	57
55	56	58
56	57	59

Lesson 7.2, page 96

	a	b
1.	70	182
2.	290	2,310
3.	65	500
4.	1,427	1,950
5.	125	5,580
6.	45	221

Lesson 7.3, page 97

	a	b	c
1.	multiply	multiply	add
2.	subtract	divide	divide
3.	add	subtract	add

	a	b
4.	10	7
5.	8	8
6.	9	1
7.	8	20
8.	10	2
9.	8	8
10.	40	40
11.	1	5
12.	32	24

Lesson 7.3, page 98

	a	b
1.	15	1
2.	18	13
3.	3	4
4.	16	11
5.	10	15
6.	7	4
7.	3	24

Lesson 7.4, page 99

1. $5 - 2$
2. $3 \times (4 + 12)$
3. $10 + 15 \div 3$
4. $2 + 6 \times 4$
5. $\frac{2}{3} \times (30 - 11)$
6. $2 \times (8 - 2)$
7. $6 \times 4 + 3 \times 4$
8. $\frac{1}{4} \times 8 + 11$

Lesson 7.4, page 100

Answers may vary.

1. the product of 3 and the sum of 2 and 8
2. 6 times the difference between 2 and $\frac{1}{6}$

Grade 5 Answers

3. the product of 5 and the sum of 3 and 5
4. the quotient of 20 and the sum of 3 and 1
5. the sum of $\frac{1}{4}$ times 8 and 11
6. the product of 12 and the sum of 3 and 5
7. the sum of 8 and 4 divided by 2
8. 9 times 4 increased by 7

Lesson 7.5, page 101
1. and – addition, how many more – subtraction; 8
2. twice – multiplication, total – addition, and – addition; 81
3. times – multiplication, total – addition; 40
4. and – addition, each – multiplication, how many more – subtraction; 28

Lesson 7.5, page 102
1. $(15 + 30 + 18) - (6 + 8) = 49$
2. $(3 \times 2) + (5 \times 4) = 26$
3. $(5 \times 4) + (6 \times 9) = 74$
4. $(\$32 + \$27 + \$38) - (\$18 + \$47) = \$32$

Posttest, page 103
1.
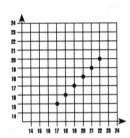

	a	b
2.	15	8
3.	7	51
4.	7	44
5.	24	68
6.	17	30
7.	4	6

Posttest, page 104
8. $11 \times (8 + 5)$
9. $6 \times (16 - 2)$
10. $\frac{1}{2} \times 8 + 6$
11. $(8 + 12) \div 4$
12. $(\$62.00 \times 8) + (\$25.50 \times 4) = \$598.00$
13. $(7 \times 8) - (7 \times 4) = 28$

Chapter 8

Pretest, page 105
	a	b
1.	2	15,840
2.	8	13,960
3.	20	48
4.	50	6,000

5. 8,000   12
6.

$1\frac{3}{4}$ miles
7. P = 20 ft., A = 24 sq. ft.   P = 28 ft., A = 39 sq. ft.

Pretest, page 106
	a	b
8.	36 cubic inches	64 cubic inches
9.	2,100	
10.	9,000	
11.	200	
12.	8 hours and 32 minutes	

Lesson 8.1, page 107
	a	b
1.	5,000	17
2.	4	51
3.	60	8,000
4.	4,000,000	46
5.	42,000	12,000
6.	2,150	4,200
7.	Duane's, 6	
8.	Pedro's, 20,700	

Lesson 8.2, page 108
	a	b
1.	4	10
2.	5	18
3.	5	32,000
4.	28	16
5.	7	128
6.	98	6
7.	32,005	9
8.	64	24
9.	252	3
10.	20	11
11.	13,801	10
12.	197	21,344
13.	9	6
14.	16	21
15.	14	12
16.	11	1,764

Lesson 8.3, page 109
1.   2.
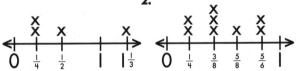

Grade 5 Answers

1. $(2 \times \frac{1}{4}) + \frac{1}{2} + 1\frac{1}{3} = 2\frac{1}{3}$;
   No, the tower will not be tall enough.
2. $(2 \times \frac{1}{4}) + (3 \times \frac{3}{8}) + (2 \times \frac{5}{6}) + \frac{5}{8} = 3\frac{11}{12}$;
   $3\frac{11}{12} \div 8 = \frac{47}{96}$; $\frac{47}{96}$ pint of water will be in each beaker.

Lesson 8.4, page 110

	a	b	c
1.	20 in.	19 yd.	32 ft.
2.	20 ft.	48 in.	24 in.
3.	19 yd.	18 yd.	12 yd.
4.	22 ft.	25 in.	40 ft.

Lesson 8.4, page 111

	a	b	c
1.	16 m	10 mm	20 cm
2.	18 km	26 cm	21 m
3.	82 mm	50 m	96 km
4.	14 cm	20 m	32 m

Lesson 8.5, page 112

	a	b	c
1.	15 sq. in.	16 sq. ft.	16 sq. ft.
2.	14 sq. yd.	49 sq. in.	6 sq. yd.
3.	64 sq. ft.	45 sq. in.	30 sq. yd.

Lesson 8.5, page 113

	a	b	c
1.	10 sq. in.	63 sq. in.	9 sq. in.
2.	40 sq. cm	16 sq. cm	24 sq. cm
3.	36 sq. cm	31 sq. in.	25 sq. cm

Lesson 8.6, page 114

1. $3 \times 3 \times 3 = 27$
2. $6 \times 4 \times 5 = 120$
3. $6 \times 8 \times 2 = 96$
4. $5 \times 5 \times 5 = 125$

Lesson 8.7, page 115

	a	b	c
1.	8 cubic in.	48 cubic yd.	15 cubic ft.
2.	36 cubic yd.	126 cubic ft.	90 cubic ft.
3.	112 cubic in.	60 cubic yd.	189 cubic ft.

Lesson 8.7, page 116

	a	b	c
1.	8 cubic cm	60 cubic m	36 cubic m
2.	42 cubic cm	144 cubic cm	54 cubic m
3.	24 cubic m	100 cubic m	216 cubic m

Lesson 8.7, page 117

	a	b
1.	288 cubic cm	264 cubic cm
2.	200 cubic m	48 cubic in.

3. 36 cubic ft. 384 cubic in.
4. 120 cubic in. 270 cubic in.
5. 120 cubic in. 288 cubic m

Lesson 8.8, page 118

1.	122 ft.	4.	1,188 cubic yd.
2.	24 sq. in.	5.	8 ft.
3.	76 ft.	6.	600 cubic in.

Lesson 8.8, page 119

1.	270 m	4.	135 sq. m
2.	9 cm	5.	24 sq. m
3.	14 km	6.	144 cubic m

Lesson 8.9, page 120

	a	b
1.	2 hr. 38 min.	10 hr. 33 min.
2.	7 hr. 5 min.	6 hr. 24 min.
3a.	12:15 a.m.; 2:51 a.m.; 2 hr. 36 min.	
3b.	3:37 a.m.; 10:35 a.m.; 6 hr. 58 min.	

Posttest, page 121

	a	b
1.	27	93
2.	34	34
3.	192	28,000
4.	16,000	636
5.	7,000,000	8,942

6.

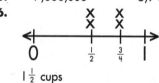

$1\frac{1}{2}$ cups

	a	b	c
7.	P = 26 ft.	P = 24 m	P = 26 m
	A = 42 sq. ft.	A = 32 sq. m	A = 33 sq. m

Posttest, page 122

	a	b
8.	45 cubic cm	18 cubic ft.
9.	8 hr. 55 min.	
10.	35 sq. yd.	
11.	30 cubic m	
12a.	8 hours and 17 minutes	
12b.	14 hours and 13 minutes	

Chapter 9

Pretest, page 123

1.
2. 1
3. 4

Grade 5 Answers

4. 3
5. 2

	a	b
6.	rectangle	triangle
7.	square	hexagon

Pretest, page 124

	a	b
8.	25°, A	140°, O
9.	150°, O	90°, R
10.	X	
11.	X	
12.	XW, XZ, XY	
13.	RT	
14.	YZ	

Lesson 9.1, page 125

1.
2.
3.
4.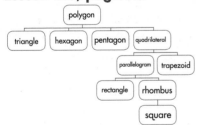

Lesson 9.2, page 126

1. A, B, F, G, L
2. B, C, F, G, M
3. D, K
4. B, F, G
5. E, H
6. B, F, G

Lesson 9.3, page 127

Lesson 9.4, page 128

	a	b
1.	acute	acute
2.	obtuse	acute
3.	right	obtuse

Lesson 9.4, page 129

	a	b
1.	∠ABC = 60°, acute	∠GHI = 90°, right
2.	∠PQR = 110°, obtuse	∠XYZ = 170°, obtuse

3.	∠123 = 90°, right	∠ABC = 30°, acute
4.	∠ABC = 60°, acute	∠XYZ = 90°, right

Lesson 9.5, page 130

	a	b	c	d
1.	diameter	chord	radius	chord
2.	O			
3.	O			
4.	$\overline{OT}$, $\overline{OS}$, $\overline{OR}$			
5.	$\overline{MN}$, $\overline{TR}$			
6.	$\overline{TR}$			

7. Answers will vary. One possible answer is shown.

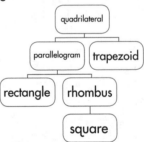

Posttest, page 131

1.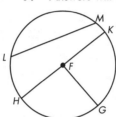
2. 2
3. 1
4. 3
5.

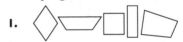

Posttest, page 132

	a	b
6.	90°, R	160°, O
7.	40°, A	120°, O
8.	S	
9.	S	
10.	$\overline{ST}$, $\overline{SR}$, $\overline{SV}$	
11.	$\overline{RV}$	
12.	$\overline{WV}$	

Pretest, page 133

	a	b
1.	(2, 7)	(6, 2)
2.	(4, 5)	(2, 2)

Grade 5 Answers

3-4.

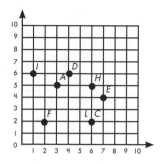

Pretest, page 134

	a	b	c
5.	S	W	U
6.	N	P	X

7.

2 units

8.

16 units

9.

11 units

10.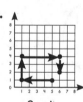

2 units

Possible solution: #9, 10.

Lesson 10.1, page 135

	a	b	c
1.	(3, 3)	(8, 2)	(2, 4)
2.			

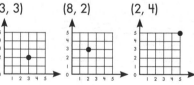

Lesson 10.2, page 136

1. J; E
2. H; G
3. L; M
4. C; K
5. F; D
6. (1, 6); (8, 8)
7. (8, 3); (6, 5)
8. (7, 1); (5, 7)
9. (1, 4); (2, 2)
10. (4, 8); (4, 1)

11-12.

Lesson 10.2, page 137

	a	b	c
1.	K	H	F
2.	B	L	E
3.	(7, 8)	(1, 6)	(2, 3)
4.	(6, 2)	(4, 3)	(6, 4)

5-6.

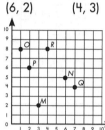

Lesson 10.3, page 138

1.	2	3.	14
2.	6	4.	12

Lesson 10.3, page 139

1. 6 blocks—2 blocks south and 4 blocks east
2. 9 blocks—4 blocks south and 5 blocks west
3. 10 blocks—6 blocks east and 4 blocks north
4. (7, 1)

Posttest, page 140

	a	b
1.	(3, 2)	(4, 5)
2.	(8, 8)	(3, 5)

3-4.

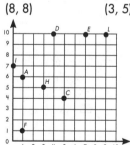

Posttest, page 141

	a	b	c
5.	F	D	L
6.	C	B	H

Grade 5 Answers

7.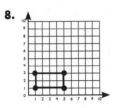

6 units

8.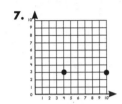

12 units

9.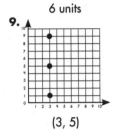

(3, 5)

10.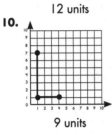

9 units

Final Test

Final Test, page 142

	a	b	c	d
1.	544	15,714	2,003,184	1,847,200
2.	134 r2	1,398 r18	58	93
3.	4.61	$87.70	$9.59	21.24
4.	261.589	60.5088	7,186.7528	4,559.052
5.	76	8.2	3.2	4.3

Final Test, page 143

	a	b	c	d
6.	$\frac{41}{60}$	$1\frac{1}{5}$	$18\frac{3}{5}$	$6\frac{5}{14}$
7.	$\frac{1}{2}$	$\frac{11}{63}$	$5\frac{5}{9}$	$3\frac{11}{12}$
8.	$\frac{2}{7}$	$\frac{3}{8}$	$\frac{7}{32}$	$\frac{9}{11}$
9.	$\frac{1}{4}$	35	$\frac{1}{36}$	21
10.	$6\frac{2}{3}$	$16\frac{9}{10}$	$12\frac{3}{5}$	8

Final Test, page 144

	a	b
11.	tenths	ten thousands
12.	hundredths	hundreds
13.	103,500	2,000,000
14.	23,000	103,700
15.	$\frac{1}{150}$, 1.5, 1.7, $\frac{8}{3}$	
16.	$\frac{2}{3}$, 0.75, $\frac{5}{6}$, 0.85	

	a	b	c
17.	$2\frac{5}{12}$	$4\frac{3}{5}$	$2\frac{1}{2}$
18.	$\frac{9}{2}$	$\frac{51}{7}$	$\frac{65}{8}$

19.

	Add 1	Add 2
30	31	32
31	32	33
32	33	34
33	34	35
34	35	36
35	36	37

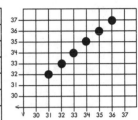

Final Test, page 145

	a	b
20.	255	9
21.	33	38

	a	b	c
22.	A = 8 sq. ft.	A = 30 sq. in.	A = 53 sq. cm
	P = 12 ft.	P = 26 in.	P = 32 cm

23a. 14 hours and 42 minutes
23b. 7 hours and 11 minutes

Final Test, page 146

	a	b	c
24.	56 cubic yd.	125 cubic ft.	72 cubic in.

25.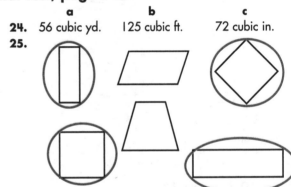

26.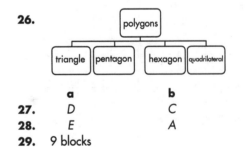

	a	b
27.	D	C
28.	E	A

29. 9 blocks